U.S. Foreign Policy and the
New International Economic Order

About the Book and Author

U.S. Foreign Policy and
the New International Economic Order:
Negotiating Global Problems, 1974–1981

Robert K. Olson

This is an up-to-date, authoritative account of the development of U.S. policy toward the New International Economic Order (NIEO) from its inception in 1974 through the Eleventh Special Session of the General Assembly in August–September 1980. Mr. Olson concentrates on the latter stages of the North-South dialogue, analyzing U.S. policy in the context of broad foreign policy objectives pursued since the end of World War II and also in light of events of the seventies and the 1980 Soviet invasion of Afghanistan. On the premise that policy is, ultimately, what happens at the negotiating table, he also specifically examines the record of U.S. negotiations on the Common Fund, UNCTAD V, and other major North-South meetings during 1979-1980. This material, together with an examination of how policy is made within the U.S. bureaucracy, who makes it, and why, provides fresh insight into a complex process.

Mr. Olson seeks to determine if and to what extent U.S. policy serves basic U.S. interests and whether the negotiating process has been an effective medium for global problem solving. He concludes that although U.S. policy and practice do serve traditional U.S. foreign policy interests, the political cost is high. He also concludes that NIEO negotiations have not been an effective means for global problem solving and that rapid change in political and economic realities has rendered obsolete the basic concepts — the very mechanisms for problem solving — on both sides.

Robert K. Olson is a retired U.S. Foreign Service officer and a former official of the U.S. Department of State. He was directly involved in the early stages of the negotiations described in this book and recently spent two years at the University of Oxford studying the diplomatic processes for global problem solving.

Future historians may view the second half of the twentieth century not so much as a power conflict between the Soviet Union and the United States, but as a period of challenge to the North Atlantic Community, thrown out by the unexpectedly rapid rise of non-Western peoples to an ever-growing voice in world affairs.

—Hans Kohn
Is the Liberal West in Decline?

U.S. Foreign Policy and the New International Economic Order:
Negotiating Global Problems, 1974–1981

Robert K. Olson

Westview Press • Boulder, Colorado
Frances Pinter Ltd • London

This volume is included in Westview Special Studies in International Relations.

Copyright © 1981 by Westview Press, Inc.

Published in 1981 in the United States of America by
  Westview Press, Inc.
  5500 Central Avenue
  Boulder, Colorado 80301
  Frederick A. Praeger, Publisher

Published in Great Britain in 1981 by
  Frances Pinter (Publishers) Limited
  5 Dryden Street, London WC2E 9NW

Library of Congress Catalog Card Number: 81-11682
ISBN (U.S.): 0-86531-125-0
ISBN (U.K.): 0-903804-95-6

Printed and bound in the United States of America

To Yvonne, with love,
and to Happy Days
at Stork Cottage

Contents

Abbreviations

ABM	antiballistic missile
ACAST	Advisory Committee for the Application of Science and Technology for Development (UN)
ACP	African, Caribbean, and Pacific (countries signatory to the Lomé Convention)
AID	Agency for International Development (U.S.)
CERDS	Charter of Economic Rights and Duties of States (UN)
CIEC	Conference on International Economic Cooperation
COW	Committee of the Whole (UNGA)
DAC	Development Assistance Committee (OECD)
DC	developed country
EB	Bureau of Economic and Business Affairs (U.S. State Department)
EC	European Community
ECDC	economic cooperation among developing countries
ECGF	export credit guarantee facility
ECOSOC	Economic and Social Council (UN)
FAO	Food and Agriculture Organization (UN specialized agency)
G-77	Group of 77: developing country economic negotiating bloc
GA	General Assembly (UN)
GAO	General Accounting Office (U.S.)
GATT	General Agreement on Tariffs and Trade
Group B	Western developed country members of UNCTAD
GSP	generalized system of preferences
GSTP	global system of trade preferences among developing countries
IAEA	International Atomic Energy Agency
IBRD	International Bank for Reconstruction and Development (World Bank)
ICA	International Commodity Agreement
IDA	International Development Association
IEA	International Energy Agency (OECD)
IFTD	international fund for trade and development

ILO	International Labour Organisation (UN specialized agency)
IMF	International Monetary Fund
IO	Bureau of International Organization Affairs (State Department)
IPC	Integrated Programme for Commodities (UNCTAD)
IWA	International Wheat Agreement
IWC	International Wheat Council
LDC	developing country (less developed country)
LLDC	least developed country
MBFR	mutual and balanced force reduction
MDB	multilateral development bank
MNE	multinational enterprise
MTN	multinational trade negotiations
NATO	North Atlantic Treaty Organization
NIEO	New International Economic Order
NTB	nontariff barrier
ODA	official development assistance
OECD	Organization for Economic Cooperation and Development
OMB	Office of Management and Budget (U.S.)
OPEC	Organization of Petroleum Exporting Countries
RBP	restrictive business practice
RDB	regional development bank
RTA	retroactive terms adjustment
R&D	research and development
SALT	Strategic Arms Limitation Talks
SDR	special drawing rights
SEATO	Southeast Asia Treaty Organization
STABEX	European Community LDC export commodity stabilization system
STO	state trading organization
S&T	science and technology
TDB	Trade and Development Board
TNC	transnational corporation
UNCSTD	UN Conference on Science and Technology for Development
UNCTAD	UN Conference on Trade and Development
UNDP	United Nations Development Program
UNESCO	United Nations Educational, Scientific, and Cultural Organization (specialized agency)
UNGA	United Nations General Assembly
UNIDO	United Nations Industrial Development Organization (specialized agency)
WCARRD	World Conference on Agrarian Reform and Rural Development
WHO	World Health Organization (UN specialized agency)
WIPO	World Intellectual Property Organization

Preface

The most pervasive factor dealt with in this study is change. During the writing of this book, the central subject, the foreign policy of the United States, has undergone a sea change following the invasion of Afghanistan, from a mood of withdrawal from overseas commitments to resumption of a global outlook and, following the 1980 elections, to a mood of confidence and self-assertion. International relations, as in the Middle East, seem constantly to fluctuate and change. We are ever aware that the world is moving inexorably into a new era dimly perceived but promising to be radically different from the present. It has become fashionable to see the times in terms of instability and revolution, and U.S. leaders have repeatedly referred to this era as one of tumult and disorder.

I have, therefore, tried to anchor this study on fundamental concepts and primary sources in which a measure of authority may be found. I have endeavored to discover continuities and constants amid the changing pattern of events. It is essential to do so, I believe; for without some baseline from which to work, the daily deluge of alarms and excursions in the world is merely a tale of "sound and fury, signifying nothing."

Nevertheless, it would be presumptuous to pretend to final authority or infallibility for my views. I can only hope to have asked the right questions and to have provided an introduction to a complex and swiftly changing subject. No one could be more aware than I am that this work can only be a tentative attempt to rough out a chapter in the diplomatic history of U.S. relations with the Third World. There is much published as opinion and much on the various substantive issues, but, as yet, very little has been published on the diplomatic dimension. A definitive history will not be written for decades, if at all, and can only result from the combined efforts of myriad students.

I am, therefore, vividly aware of the debt owed to others working on related aspects of this field. It would be impossible to name them, and the literature is so vast that the bibliography can only be suggestive. However, I feel constrained to mention the work of organizations like the Overseas Development Council in Washington, D.C., and the Overseas Development Institute in London, which consistently produce intelligent, timely, and balanced studies of aspects of the North-South dialogue.

I wish to express my thanks to those whose names do not appear in the bibliography. They are the officers and staffs of the Department of State and of U.S. missions and embassies abroad and the officers and staffs of UNCTAD, UN agencies, and the Commonwealth Secretariat, who have, without exception, given generously of their time and physical resources. I also wish to note that, again without exception, none have betrayed to me any partisan feelings or provided one-sided views as might reasonably have been expected. None showed resentment over North-South differences; rather, all displayed a professional understanding of the problems and of the difficulties of working them out in a world of men and institutions.

Nothing, therefore, should suggest that the views expressed or any errors of fact or interpretation are other than my own. In no case has anyone tried to influence my judgment. I have portrayed events as they appeared to me, sedulously drawing my own conclusions and preferring to live with my own mistakes.

I am deeply grateful to the University of Oxford for providing the incomparable atmosphere and facilities without which this work could never have been undertaken. Particular thanks go to Professor Hedley Bull, Balliol College, whose gentle guidance and advice proved to be invaluable and infallibly correct; to C.I.W. Seton-Watson, Fellow of Oriel, for his cheerful hospitality and assistance; to the staffs of Queen Elizabeth House and the Bodleian Library; and to friends and colleagues who, each in his or her own way, helped to make residence at Oxford pleasant as well as productive.

But it is appropriate that the final pages of this study should be written in Washington, D.C., a very different place from Oxford, a city where change is the basic and dominating fact of life. Here the past is merely prologue so that this book is, at best, but an introduction to another already being written by the new administration. Already the Reagan team has proposed sweeping changes in North-South philosophy and policy, which mark a sharp break with those of the Carter administration so that even my conclusions are only a preface.

R.K.O.
Washington, D.C.

Introduction

During the early seventies, the traditional concerns of foreign relations — bilateral political and economic relations — began to give way to, even in the operational sense to be overwhelmed by, a wave of global issues such as the problems and consequences of population growth, food and energy shortages, economic imbalances, poverty, environmental degradation, and atomic proliferation. At the same time, it became apparent that the traditional machinery and institutions of international relations were not designed to cope with generalized problems of such magnitude, nor were most of the leaders equipped with the intellectual concepts and moral perceptions needed to cope with them constructively. Nevertheless, the decade generated many serious recommendations and attempts to cope with many of these problems.

The North-South dialogue between the industrialized nations and the developing nations is one of the major efforts to deal with some of these problems. It may not be comprehensive, but it is a key element among such efforts as it does involve food, population, energy, the environment, the world economy, and many more fundamental economic, social, and political issues. The Third World proposal for a New International Economic Order (NIEO) has become the central issue around which the dialogue has revolved — or raged (for a fuller explanation of the NIEO, see Chapter 4). The NIEO proposal, launched in 1974 in the United Nations, includes almost all aspects of the North-South dialogue but with an interpretation of the world political economy that has crystallized attitudes — North and South — into seemingly irreconcilable positions. The Third World claims that the world economy continues to exploit the developing nations for the benefit of the developed; that despite a quarter century of development assistance, the gap between the rich and the poor is increasing, and that nothing less than a new international economic order is required to change the trend. The developed countries reject both the diagnosis and the cure. Nevertheless, the dialogue continues in the search for common solutions to what are truly common problems. The extent to which it succeeds or fails is of profound importance to all.

I have concentrated on the U.S. role. The United States, because of its size and influence, has been the crucial factor in determining how and to what extent this historic and multifaceted process will develop and progress, assuming the process is amenable to direction at all. No single power can effectively channel or dominate the tides of change now flowing, but the role of the United States is decisive to any collective effort. Indeed, the key to North-South matters lies on the banks of the Potomac if it lies anywhere. Of central importance, therefore, is knowing what U.S. interests and the policies designed to serve those interests are. I have tried to define U.S. policy toward the NIEO from two points of view: (1) as an expression of broad U.S. policy interests and (2) as the record of U.S. performance at North-South negotiations. By relating the two aspects of U.S. policy, the conceptual and the pragmatic, I hope to produce a coherent picture of U.S. policy toward the NIEO as it has developed during the latter half of the decade of the seventies and to determine whether U.S. practices at negotiations have been supportive of U.S. interests.

Finally, the book draws these two principal factors, the NIEO and U.S. policy, into a coherent account and follows their relationships through the major negotiations of the past half decade. In so doing, I hope to shed some light on the dynamics of the North-South dialogue and the problems or obstacles faced in attempting to solve global problems through the mechanism of multilateral negotiations.

Methodology

I have taken the historical or sequential approach on the premise that foreign policy is best understood in its historical context. There has been a good deal written about international relations from the functional point of view and a good deal of functional thinking — some useful, some nonsensical — by policy analysts in and out of government. For example, in trying to deal with global issues as functional problems, we are reminded that these issues or problems are not abstract but turn up at the negotiating table as peoples and nations, as rights, obligations, and ideologies, and as debts and disasters. It is in those terms, ultimately, that solutions have to be molded.

I have, nevertheless, resorted to analysis in order to discern the reality behind the rhetoric of North-South affairs. The study therefore examines the North-South dialogue, not as arguments over conflicting social and economic systems, but as negotiations. That is, my analysis is based on the premise that a country's real policy is what it does at the negotiating table rather than what it professes to do in public statements, however well intended. The perceptions and the dynamics of negotiation erase some features and emphasize others, frequently producing a quite different result than what is presented to the public or even planned for.

Parameters

The natural time span of this study seems to be the decade of the seventies during which time the spotlight was on global issues and the North-South dialogue. The decade of the seventies was also a period of coherence in American life, a period of withdrawal from overseas commitments and a period with a special flavor and nature of its own. Because of the importance of the United States, the fortunes of the North-South dialogue cannot be properly evaluated without recognizing the American attitudes that were prevalent during the period.

It is impossible to do justice to a whole decade in a study of this size, and no attempt has been made to do so; the history of the North-South dialogue has yet to be written. This work concentrates on Phase 2 of the dialogue, from the special meeting of Third World leaders in December 1975 at Arusha through September 1980 and the Eleventh Special Session of the General Assembly, although earlier events are summarized in the opening chapters. Rather than to attempt to cover the whole range of North-South events and issues, I have focused on the negotiations at UNCTAD V, which cover the central aspects of the NIEO.

Neither does this study attempt to address the traditional aspects of U.S. policy — development assistance, security assistance, and food aid — that constitute the principal U.S. economic and political commitments to Third World countries. These programs do get entangled and confused with the NIEO and its aims and objectives, but they are not central to it. The NIEO is primarily concerned with trade and the working of the international economic order. The U.S. response to that concern is what this book is about.

Sources

With regard to the negotiations, I have relied almost entirely on official records — documents, position papers, reports, communications, and studies produced by the U.S. government and international organizations. This material has been supplemented by interviews with U.S. officials in Washington, D.C., Geneva, London, and Brussels, who have been involved in the formulation of policy and have represented the United States in negotiations. Readers may question the frequent reference to "official sources" with no further information given. This type of citation has been required by the Department of State in lieu of specific documentary references that could not be cited or in cases where individuals did not wish to have their names used. I have based the analysis of U.S. interests on published statements of key administration officials.

I have also drawn on a wide range of published material. This includes books, articles, and monographs by reputable scholars and former officials, such as George Ball and Senator Daniel P. Moynihan; materials produced by news media and the UN, UNCTAD, the IMF, and the World Bank were also consulted. I make no claim to originality for those sections that are based on this secondary material, except, perhaps, in the arrangement of ideas. Nor do I make any claim to have exhausted all available material, tested every hypothesis, or evaluated every judgment. To have done so would not, in any case, have been relevant since the basic argument of the work stands on primary sources not hitherto evaluated.

Organization

The organization of the book follows from an attempt to answer two basic questions: Does U.S. policy, as carried out, support basic U.S. interests? and Have negotiations in the NIEO been an effective process for global problem solving? Chapter 1 describes the origin and development of U.S. foreign policy interests during the post–World War II era and the impact of the crises of the seventies and the Third World challenge exemplified by the NIEO. Chapter 2 traces U.S. policy toward the NIEO during Phase 1 of the dialogue, which ended in 1978, and Chapter 3 introduces Phase 2 of the dialogue — the preparations for UNCTAD V and the reiteration of established policy on the part of the North and the South. Chapter 4 analyzes in detail the UNCTAD V negotiations across the broad range of the NIEO. Chapter 5 traces post–UNCTAD V events, including the World Conference on Agrarian Reform and Rural Development (WCARRD), the UN Conference on Science and Technology for Development (UNCSTD), proposals to convene a new round of comprehensive negotiations, and the Sixth Non-Aligned Summit in Havana in September 1979. Chapter 6 follows the events of 1979–1980, from the Thirty-fourth General Assembly to the Eleventh Special Session, including an account of the effects of the Soviet invasion of Afghanistan, of the Third Conference of the United Nations Industrial Development Organization (UNIDO III), and of the Venice Summit. Chapter 7 provides an integrated account of U.S. policy toward the NIEO in the light of overall U.S. foreign policy interests and the record of negotiations and examines how, why, and by whom that policy is made.

U.S. Policy and the Third World: The Postwar Era

To understand U.S. policy toward the NIEO, one must see it in the wider context of world events, especially of U.S. foreign policy since World War II. The NIEO negotiations may be unique in many ways, but they are, nevertheless, only the latest episode of a relationship toward the Third World that goes back many years. The history, dynamics, and evolving nature of this relationship has had a life of its own, which directly affects the question of the NIEO. In a phrase, it may be seen as a record of a basically liberal U.S. policy distorted and sometimes overshadowed by even more-powerful political, economic, and military considerations. Thus, throughout the era, there has been a tug-of-war among competing objectives and interests in which special Third World interests have had to compete.

U.S. Interests and the Postwar World

The basic U.S. attitude toward Third World countries is derived from Wilsonian liberalism and the principle of self-determination of nations and an overt dislike of empire and what it stood for. Self-determination, in a simplistic way, is embodied in the Declaration of Independence and was the very principle for which the American colonies fought the Revolution. In 1941 Franklin D. Roosevelt and Winston Churchill bickered over the phrasing of the Atlantic Charter — whether and to what extent it applied outside Europe — and Americans were outspoken about their reluctance to die to preserve the British Empire (as they saw it). Presidential candidate Wendell Willkie, during his 1942 world tour, declared that the war must mean the "end of the empire of nations over other nations." Churchill, provoked, declared that he had "not become the King's first Minister in order to preside over the liquidation of the British Empire."[1]

U.S. opposition to empire was not only political but economic as U.S. negotiators, haunted by the depression of the thirties and the need to find markets for a greatly enlarged U.S. productive capacity after the war, concentrated on making an open-trading world. It was thought that not only are closed economic blocs inefficient and protectionist, but they develop into competing political blocs. This philosophy was embodied in Article IV of the Atlantic Charter and in the 1944 Bretton Woods agreement that set up the international monetary system. In 1945, in return for a $3.8-billion loan from the United States, the United Kingdom wearily agreed to dismantle its imperial trading system. France, to Charles De Gaulle's consternation, was forced to accept the same conditions.[2]

But this strategy for the creation of an open postwar world was quickly checked after 1945 by Soviet power in Europe and, increasingly, in the Third World. The Cold War began in Europe, but by 1949, it had spread to the Pacific and swept over the countries of the Asian perimeter from Greece to Korea. Defense of the free world became the principal objective of U.S. foreign policy.

Those three elements—political self-determination or national independence, an open world-trading system, and collective security against Soviet communism—became the United States' basic international interests after the war and they provided the framework for U.S. foreign policy, including relations with the Third World in the years to follow. However, they were and still are only guideposts or ideals rather than absolutes or unvarying standards; inevitably, they are subordinate to practical realities, but not uniformly so. The U.S. commitment to an open, free-market economy has often been tempered by unilateral trade and monetary restrictions to meet some temporary exigency. Opposition to communism has been modified as perceptions changed, the "monolith" broke apart, and détente developed. But those changes have been more of degree than of kind. The commitment to Third World "independence," however, has been equivocal and confused.

The commitment to the ideal of Third World independence was difficult to live up to. The United States did put pressure on the Netherlands to grant Indonesia independence after the war but refrained from interfering directly in relations between the United Kingdom and France and their colonial dependencies. As the Cold War deepened, solidarity with U.S. allies took priority over the commitment to independence. Indeed, the United States eventually found itself filling the power vacuum left by the withdrawal of European authority in Southeast Asia and the Middle East. In doing so, it slipped out of the role of the liberator and protector of new nations and became, increasingly in the eyes of the Third World elites, the neocolonial oppressor. Only during the Suez crisis in 1956 did the United

States allow Third World interests to come between it and its NATO allies. Similarly, the commitment to Third World independence was soon overshadowed by the growth of the international economy and the interests of the multinational corporations, causing Third World nations to complain that political domination had merely been replaced by economic domination and that true independence could come only from a more equitable international economic order.

Nevertheless, fostering and protecting the political independence of new nations in the Third World has remained an official "ideal," whether it emerges as direct support for a specific country, as aid for development, or as a warning against Soviet intervention. Not least important, U.S. policymakers, politicians, and people believe the ideal to be an article of faith expressing a deep-seated intention, however imperfectly applied. Third World complaints and Marxist denunciations have baffled and hurt Americans who, rather than feeling guilty for having "exploited" Third World countries as charged, have been proud of their aid and friendship.

U.S. policy during the postwar period should be viewed as an interplay between ideal objectives and pragmatic actions designed to meet practical, and usually pressing, objectives, some of which have achieved an almost permanent status. For instance, aid was originally conceived of as a temporary expedient that would become unnecessary after postwar economic recovery. U.S. policy must also be seen as the result of rivalry among the three main interests, each of which has become institutionalized in Washington, with its own bureaucratic machinery and its own political support structure in Congress and in the country. History presents the interplay as a series of events.

In early postwar years there was turmoil from Indonesia to North Africa as nationalist movements clashed with colonial powers and fought among themselves. If the turmoil did not bring the millenium for the new nations themselves, it did highlight dramatically the importance of the Third World for Western interests. The situation was strangely like the present one. U.S. Assistant Secretary of State Will Clayton observed in November 1946 that "the expansion in the domestic economy and the depletion of our national resources would make the United States much more dependent on imports of raw materials and minerals, many from the newly emerging areas."[3] Also in 1946, Adolph Berle — economist, adviser to Roosevelt and Truman, and State Department official — declared that the Soviet Union and the United States had begun a battle for the allegiance of the less-industrialized nations and that U.S. productivity must be used to take the lead in the material reconstruction of the newly emerging countries.[4] Greece was locked in a civil war with Communist insurgents, Turkey was under heavy Soviet pressure, and in early 1946, the Soviets appeared to be digging in rather than withdrawing from Iran. It was a time of testing, uncertainty, and reevaluation as the wartime vision of an orderly, a cooperative, and an open world was displaced by hard political fact.

On March 12, 1947, in a message to Congress, President Harry Truman finally issued his declaration of Cold War, which became known as the Truman Doctrine. In that message and in an earlier speech at Baylor University on March 6, Truman spelled out the political and economic parameters of U.S. interests in the postwar world. The free world was threatened by Soviet communism, he said, not just in Europe and the Near East but worldwide. If it was not stopped and if an open world economy were not restored, depression would occur. Peace, freedom, and world trade were indivisible. Truman urged the United States to commit itself to helping "free peoples" and to opposing "totalitarian regimes."[5]

This enunciation of the Truman Doctrine was followed by direct aid to Greece and Turkey and by the Marshall Plan in March 1948. The next year there was the then glamorous Point Four Program, which called for providing scientific and industrial knowledge to the newly emerging na-tions—the beginning of the U.S. development assistance program. Even then aid programs met with considerable opposition from the business world, which would have preferred treaties that ensured fair and equitable treatment for private investment to interference from the U.S. government and the United Nations (which was to administer the aid program). It was 1950 before Congress grudgingly passed a $27-million aid bill, which still put aid on a temporary basis subject to annual review.

Aid nevertheless became a constant factor in U.S. foreign relations, sub-ject to a variety of uses and abuses by both donor and recipient. And, for better or worse, aid became one of the main channels of official Third World relations; the cure-all for poverty, political instability, and dissatisfaction; the easy answer to all problems; a justification for pro-moting U.S. interests; and, inevitably, a constant bone of contention be-tween donor and recipient. During a period of profound change and unrest, aid programs also served to distract attention from political realities. Ultimately, the philosophy was to wear thin, and Third World na-tions were to shift from asking for more aid to wanting better terms of trade, as is exemplified in the demand for a new international economic order.

The decade of the fifties fulfilled Truman's worst predictions as South Asia, from east to west, became a battleground of the Cold War, with each superpower bent on winning over the newly independent nations. By 1956 Chairman Nikita Khrushchev had negotiated fourteen economic and military assistance agreements in the "zone of liberation" from North Africa to Southeast Asia,[6] and the United States had negotiated the Baghdad Pact in the Middle East and had formed the Southeast Asia Treaty Organization (SEATO). At the NATO foreign ministers' meeting in 1956, Secretary of State John Foster Dulles stated that communism was on the march in Asia. The West must never surrender those nations, he said; the stakes were too high. With the West's dependence on broad markets and access to raw materials, losing the Asian nations to communism would be intolerable.[7]

That policy made sense, and the United States was united behind it. The 1956 election campaign even saw a consensus between the political parties that the underdeveloped world was becoming the focus of the Cold War. The Suez crisis of October 1956, whatever else it meant, drove the point home. The result was the Eisenhower Doctrine of March 1957 that extended military and economic aid and, if necessary, committed U.S. forces to any nation requesting such aid to fight against Communist-instigated armed aggression. Within a year, President Camille Chamoun of Lebanon was calling for help as a Muslim revolution tore his country apart, but it was not until the "infiltration" of external "subversives" could be proved that the United States finally sent in the Marines.

In those days, the United States tended to believe that countries not outwardly committed to the Western camp were allies or potential allies of the Soviets and the Chinese. Communism was seen as a monolith and mere socialism as a step in the wrong direction. The U.S. aid program continued to receive liberal support but became subordinated to great-power political interests. And the Third World, caught between the superpowers, began to grope toward a philosophy of its own that was anticolonial, independent, and eventually non-aligned.[8] That groping a quarter of a century ago was the beginning of the subject with which this study is primarily concerned.

John F. Kennedy launched the decade of the sixties with a ringing declaration to "support any friend," to "oppose any foe," "to bear any burden" in the defense of liberty.[9] In a special message to Congress in May 1961, he said that the great battleground for the defense and expansion of freedom was in Asia, Latin America, Africa, and the Middle East—the "lands of the rising peoples." Kennedy restated the Truman and Eisenhower doctrines but with flair, exuberance, and imagination. Young people were told to "ask not what your country can do for you, ask what you can do for your country" and were recruited into the new Peace Corps. A grandiose Alliance for Progress was launched to make up for years of neglect and indifference toward Latin America. The aid program was given new impetus.

But Kennedy, like his predecessors and those presidents to follow, was soon overwhelmed by the "struggle" itself—by Berlin, Castro and Cuba, the Bay of Pigs, the need to plug the missile "gap," and the deterioration in Southeast Asia. Fighting communism was a full-time job, for the United

States and the Soviet Union faced each other in a contest of wills along the southern rim of Asia, in the newly independent nations of Africa, and in the Caribbean. Training of antiguerrilla forces to counter Communist revolution began at Fort Bragg and in the Canal Zone. Southeast Asia became the focus, and Kennedy declared that South Vietnam was the "cornerstone to liberty in Southeast Asia, that it was vital to keep Southeast Asia open and free from domination."[10]

The U.S. concept was ambitious, and it was grand; it ended badly. The United States got bogged down in Vietnam and became increasingly at odds not only with the Third World but with U.S. allies. Turbulence at home—the civil rights movement, black riots, the youth revolt, the assassinations of John Kennedy, Martin Luther King, and Robert Kennedy—turned the attention of Americans away from the world and inward toward their own troubles. The Tet offensive in February 1968 and the anti-Vietnam demonstrations that followed led to President Lyndon Johnson's withdrawing from the 1968 election race. The United States was already experiencing serious economic and monetary imbalances. The long retreat was beginning. Henry Kissinger and Richard Nixon, perceiving that the era of U.S. preponderance was over, concentrated on establishing a balance among the great powers, overlooking and neglecting developments in the Third World. The decade that had begun with a trumpet call ended with the Nixon Doctrine, which put a full stop to the era of open-ended involvement in the Third World.

The Seventies: The System in Crisis

The seventies have to be considered separately, for they were a turning point not only for the United States but for the world. Kissinger may have known what he was about, but in the early seventies, after twenty-five years of U.S. leadership, the world still took U.S. predominance as a given, permanent feature of the world landscape. It is doubtful if even Kissinger could have perceived in advance how the coming years were to chip, or rather hammer, away at the basic U.S. political, strategic, and economic interests on which the postwar system had been built. Unexpected and unavoidable, the changes came as a series of shocks that few people really understood and for which no one was prepared.

To confuse the picture further, the seventies ushered in a new era of "globalism." Not that the world had not been working on a global basis for generations, but suddenly every event, every issue was projected against a worldwide screen, demanding nothing less than global organizations and action for their solution. How this new outlook came about with such sudden force is unclear, but there are possible explanations. It may have begun with the picture from outer space, which showed the earth as a beautiful blue-green ball revolving serenely in the void; when mankind for the first time could actually see the world as a whole, could reflect on the artificiality of political barriers. The United Nations was becoming a global theater, the only official body with a worldwide perspective. The Swedish ambassador to the United Nations, Sverker Åström, inspired by Rolf Edberg's beautiful and disturbing book on the environment, *On the Shred of a Cloud* (1966), proposed a UN conference on the environment, which met in Stockholm in 1972. In 1973, Secretary Kissinger sought some positive focus for his speech to the Twenty-eighth General Assembly and proposed that a World Food Conference be held in Rome in 1974. A World Population Conference was already in preparation. The trend was starting, leading to a series of world conferences during the seventies on women, habitat, desertification, water, agrarian reform, and technology for development. In 1968, the Club of Rome had begun to discuss the need for a clear understanding of the working of the global system, and its first well-known study, *The Limits to Growth* prepared by Donella Meadows et al., was published in 1972. Almost imperceptibly, international preoccupation shifted from independence to interdependence, which was brought home with a vengeance during the 1973 oil crisis.

The impact of this new and stunning intellectual perspective cannot be overestimated. It produced a new, global-minded generation that would not be satisfied with anything less than instant solutions to every human problem, effected worldwide and simultaneously. The old system and its priorities, interests, and realities became instantly dated, suspect, and sometimes dysfunctional. Governments, international organizations, and officials found themselves worrying about a new range of problems for which they were ill-prepared by training and ill-equipped institutionally. The new preoccupation brought with it, inevitably, confusion, distortion, disorientation, and conflict as well as a new vision of a "better" world. It also has had an enormous impact on the ambitions, objectives, and demands of the Third World. But the United States, instead of responding with imaginative and cooperative leadership, was preoccupied with extricating itself from the mire of Vietnam.

Troubles seldom come singly, and with the advent of the seventies, the United States found itself obliged, at last, to pay for the costs of the sixties. The United States had been overspending for years, but the world's faith in the dollar was so profound that the beginning of the payments deficits in 1959 had passed unnoticed. A dollar outflow was taken for granted; dollars had provided the liquidity for rebuilding Europe and Japan, and a constant dollar outflow had been essential to bridge the "dollar gap" as those countries bought heavily to get back on their feet. But, during the sixties, the outflow became a torrent as U.S. business invested heavily abroad, affluent Americans traveled in increasing numbers, and military expenditures swelled. In 1969 the balance of trade turned against the United States as well.[11]

U.S. business also generated resentment abroad as it began to invest heavily in key economic sectors, mainly in Europe and Canada. In Canada, Pierre Elliott Trudeau was swept into power on a wave of Canadian nationalism and resentment against U.S. domination of the Canadian economy. But it was France that brought the issue to a head after the U.S. takeover of Machines Bull, France's only computer company. In February 1965, de Gaulle attacked the "privileged" position of the dollar, called for a return to the gold standard, and began to redeem dollars at Fort Knox. His actions started a trend, and during the rest of that decade, central banks, companies with dollar holdings, and speculators proceeded to buy German marks, Swiss francs, Japanese yen — and gold. U.S. gold holdings dropped alarmingly while the payments imbalance worsened. In August 1971, after a first-half-year outflow of $12.5 billion, Nixon announced that the United States would no longer redeem currency at the fixed price of gold.[12] That was the first Nixon "shock," and the world reacted with dismay and confusion. What was the dollar worth? No one knew for sure. U.S. tourists abroad were treated to the novel experience of being unable to change their dollars into local currency. The whole intricate web of monetary exchange had been struck at its most sensitive point — trust.

Fearing a return to the protectionism of the thirties, governments embarked on a hasty salvage operation. European finance ministers met with U.S. Treasury Secretary John Connally in Rome in December 1971 to negotiate new currency levels. "What would the gentlemen's reply be," asked Connally, "if I suggested a devaluation of 10%?"[13] The ministers were stunned, for with that cool offer came the dethronement of the "almighty dollar." The Bretton Woods system was finished and there was nothing to take its place. Soon added to the insecurity of the great financial powers were the frantic demands of vulnerable developing countries (LDCs) for monetary reform, stability, and a greater voice in the system.

Hard on the heels of the monetary crisis came the food crisis. During 1972 the Soviet Union negotiated enormous contracts for the purchase of food grains amounting to 950–1,000 million bushels. The bulk of what it purchased came from the United States, and U.S. supplies that were not otherwise committed were cleaned out. Unfortunately, drought had caused poor harvests in Asia and Africa, and severe hardship to millions of people. The result was a totally unexpected world shortage of food grains, which sent prices sky-high and drastically increased meat and bakery prices in the United States. While Agriculture Secretary Earl Butz toured the United

States trying to convince the angry housewife that she had never before been better off, the administration was forced, unilaterally, to curb exports. This second Nixon "shock" raised cries of protest, especially from the Japanese who depended heavily on the United States for food.

It is difficult to recall the sense of shock produced by the tangible evidence of a food shortage not only in the developing countries and the Soviet Union but in the Western industrialized nations. After thirty-odd years of plenty, the shortage was a rude jolt. How could it happen? There was, in fact, no real threat to the United States or other Western nations, but the situation opened people's eyes and provoked a battle in Washington between the free-market advocates and the stewards of food aid, international security, and concessional sales.

Meanwhile, the specter of hunger once more began to cast its shadow across the developing world. There was nothing abstract about the food question in India, where food riots followed the bad harvest, or in the Sahel, where drought-stricken nomads clustered along the southern fringe of their wasted grazing land, watching their herds die and waiting for starvation. The food shortage raised again the inevitable moral question, How can the rich third of the world's people live in opulence while the other two-thirds live on the margin of poverty with over half a billion people actually at the starvation level?

It is in the nature of the crises of the seventies that their effects were not only deranging and profound but they also acquired a life of their own. In other words, the crises were only the symptoms of far greater and more fundamental problems that called into question the very structures of the international order and of the economic system.

The 1973 Oil Crisis and Negotiations

The same month that Secretary Kissinger called for a World Food Conference, October 1973, the Egyptians launched the fourth Arab-Israeli war on Yom Kippur, the Jewish holy day, with a devastating surprise attack. Resupply of the decimated Israeli forces became an immediate necessity, and the United States responded with an emergency airlift to Israel. The Arab oil-exporting countries retaliated by imposing restraints on oil production and on the supply of oil to those consumer nations that gave support to Israel. The restraints created a sudden energy crisis, and another wave of alarm swept through the West like those of the 1971 monetary crisis and the 1972 food crisis. The fact that the United States was instrumental in precipitating all three crises was not overlooked. By the end of the year, the Organization of Petroleum Exporting Countries (OPEC) had quadrupled the price of oil in a long-overdue, but nonetheless shocking, adjustment to market realities and finite supplies. In Sheikh Ahmad Zaki Yamani's words, oil had become a "noble element."

Secondary effects rippled through the Western community. President Nixon called for a crash program to achieve energy self-sufficiency and tried to enlist the support of Europe. This had been the administration's "year of Europe," as a response to growing resentment in Europe that the United States had put European interests behind those of Asia and great power politics, but the "year of Europe" came too late. Instead of cooperating, Europe and Japan, which were more vulnerable, took a pro-Arab stand on the war and refused to aid the U.S. airlift. At that time, the United States imported only 12 percent of its oil from the Middle East, while Europe imported 80 percent of its oil and Japan, 90 percent. But Kissinger was furious and bitterly criticized the behavior of the European countries as "craven and contemptible." Not only had the "year of Europe" turned to ashes, but the secretary of state believed that Europe had become his "deepest problem."[14]

The oil price increase—up from $1.80 to $2.48 per barrel in December 1972 to over $10 in December 1973—plunged importers into serious imbalance.[15] The cost of oil imports increased in 1974 by $15 billion in the United States, by $34.4 billion in Europe, and by $12.5 billion in Japan. Hardest hit of all because they could least afford the increase were the developing countries; their import bills jumped $10 billion, increasing the cost to non-OPEC LDCs by an average 17.8 percent.[16]

The energy crisis also led to a flurry of diplomatic activity. During the two-year interval between the outbreak of the war in October 1973 and the convening of the Paris negotiations (Conference on International Economic Cooperation—CIEC) in December 1975, negotiations concerning oil formed, dissolved, and reformed again like eddies in a swift-moving stream. For the United States and Europe, the crisis was the mirror image of the Suez crisis nearly twenty years before, with the French-British and U.S. roles reversed. Surely the ghosts of Guy Mollet, Anthony Eden, and Gamal Abdel Nasser hovered over the green baize tables in Paris and Geneva. To the Third World, those years were a moment of triumph; for once, it had the upper hand, and it was determined to force, once and for all, a better deal out of the grudging West.

Nixon had announced that the United States would strive to become self-sufficient in oil. Kissinger later proposed the idea of a consumers' cartel, a petroleum importers' organization to control demand in the vain belief that a decline in demand would break OPEC. The idea was bound to fail, but the Washington Energy Conference of February 1974 did eventually lead to the formation of the International Energy Agency (IEA), which adopted an energy allocation scheme and a program for conservation, cooperation, research, and stockpiling aimed at reducing oil dependence.[17]

But the issue was far from settled by the creation of the IEA. The real answer was not just cooperation among the oil-consuming countries but a modus vivendi between producer and consumer—between OPEC and the West. On that point, the United States and France were at loggerheads. From the beginning, the United States had been opposed to any form of negotiation with OPEC and, indeed, had been discussing publicly the possible use of military power to assure access to supplies.[18] That position was a reflection of the United States outrage and shock against OPEC, its European allies, and its own impotence rather than clear diplomatic judgment, and it shocked European leaders in turn.[19] Kissinger cried "foul" when the nine members of the European Community (EC) proposed to meet with the Arab oil exporters, and he demanded that the European countries at least get prior agreement from Washington.[20]

France, on the other hand, refused to accept U.S. leadership and the Washington conference decision to create the IEA (which France never joined). France, which has nothing if not a mind of its own, was motivated by two objectives of equal importance. In the first place, France believed that Europe must reduce its dependence on U.S. leadership and had already succeeded in winning a special relationship with the Arabs, which France wished to use during the crisis to carve out a special relationship for Europe that would exclude the United States. Second, France adhered to the sound diplomatic idea of negotiating with the oil exporters.[21] The other members of the EC managed to pursue a middle course between the two extremes, convincing the United States that there was no realistic alternative to negotiations, and insisting on U.S. participation in them.

The Assault from the Third World

Meanwhile, all but unnoticed by the United States, the Third World had been hard at work constructing the concepts and language for a new international economic order. The Third World countries believed that they had largely failed to benefit under the old system and that they were falling even further behind. Therefore, the only solution was to replace the old order with a new one. In the winter of 1973–1974, encouraged by the success of the oil exporters and with the West on the defensive, the Third World movement of the Non-Aligned countries took the initiative in a diplomatic challenge to the Western system that would be fought out for the rest of the decade.

The two sides, North and South, met head-on at the Sixth Special Session of the General Assembly in April 1974 with Algerian Foreign Minister Abdulaziz Bouteflika presiding. It was a bitter clash characterized by acrimonious debate, Third World solidarity, and hard-line opposition from the United States and most of the other developed countries. The Third World laid out its demands for economic reform called the New International Economic Order (NIEO), which was designed to give the Third World an "equitable" share of the world's economic growth. It became the foundation for a campaign that is still going on and a rallying cry for the Third World.

The Declaration on the Establishment of a New International Economic Order reads like the American Declaration of Independence. It observes that new nations have come into existence since the end of World War II, and states that the peoples of those nations, having joined the "community of free peoples," are entitled to equity, sovereign equality, and interdependence. However, the international system continues to hinder their full emancipation and their progress in realizing development aims. The gap between developed and developing nations continues to grow, but the interests of both are related, and the prosperity of each is bound up with the prosperity of the whole. Therefore, a New International Economic Order must be formed, based on twenty principles. These principles stress, inter alia, sovereign equality, cooperation of all states in overcoming economic disparities, special attention to development problems, self-determination in choosing economic systems, full national control over resources, rights of restitution for exploitation, regulation of transnational corporations, national liberation wherever appropriate, just prices for developing-country exports, aid without strings, reform of the international monetary system, nonreciprocal trade preferences, and access to the achievements of science and technology — a huge order.

The United States, particularly, was opposed to many of the principles. The mood in Washington was that the United States was being steamrollered, which it was. Accustomed to taking pride in its historic stand for liberation from colonization, its pioneering work in development assistance, and its twenty-year contribution to the recovery of the world from World War II, the United States recoiled from the NIEO Declaration with bitterness and resentment. It had come as another international "insult" after the debacle in the Middle East and the defeat in Vietnam. Americans were beginning to feel isolated and betrayed on every hand, and they could not understand why. Henry Kissinger, the one man who might have provided the leadership for an appropriate response, already had a record of giving low priority to Third World affairs; he was preoccupied, in any case, with the oil crisis and shuttle diplomacy in the Middle East.

For the Third World the declaration was a tour de force. As with most significant achievements, it did not emerge suddenly in April 1974 but as the consequence of long preparation, thought, and planning to which the developed world had, hitherto, given little serious attention. In fact, behind the NIEO lay twenty years of work, "during which time the developing countries slowly constructed a network of institutions, communications and norms of diplomatic behavior that prepared them to react instantly and with such unified precision in the final months of 1973 and thereafter."[22] Behind this organizational evolution was a conceptual revolution. Henceforth, Third World demands would be based, not on the conscience of the rich, but on the idea of a world out of balance.[23]

Two separate Third World groups, with initially disparate objectives, provided the base for the 1973–1974 diplomatic explosion. The first was the Non-Aligned group, which met officially for the first time in 1961.[24] Over the years, its platform evolved from having a principally political orientation to one of economic reform, resembling in great measure the goals of the second group, the Group of 77 (G-77). The latter group had been associated with the establishment of the UN Conference on Trade and Development (UNCTAD) in 1964, and it had become the LDC economic negotiating bloc. As a result of the work of these two groups, the conceptual groundwork, the programmatic elements, the diplomatic contacts, and the norms of southern bargaining behavior vis-à-vis the countries of the Organization for Economic Cooperation and Development (OECD) were already advanced.[25]

The two groups joined forces at the Sixth Special Session of the General Assembly, but that was just the culmination of a period of intense activity under the driving leadership of Algeria, which held the chairmanship of the Non-Aligned Coordinating Bureau. Algerian preparations for the September 1973 Non-Aligned Summit in Algiers had been extraordinary. For nearly two months at an isolated resort, Algeria's "best and brightest" devoted their energies to preparing the summit papers while their normal government responsibilities languished. They built on themes already articulated by previous ministerial meetings of the G-77 and the Non-Aligned, the UNCTAD Secretariat, and the Lusaka Declaration (Third Non-Aligned Summit, September 1970). When the delegations of all seventy-five full-member states arrived in Algiers, they received a massive collection of documents including draft texts for a proposed declaration, resolutions of the conference, and a proposed action program for economic cooperation. These documents eventually became the starting drafts for the Sixth Special Session and, with a few changes, became the text of the Declaration on the Establishment of a New International Economic Order.[26]

But the final acts of the summit were more than a catalog of demands assembled by the Algerian bureaucracy; after passing through the conference, the acts represented a balanced bargain that included the priority interests of all of the regions. The Arabs gained African support for their anti-Israel plank in exchange for Arab support in African affairs and financial aid to liberation movements. Cuba's stand on Puerto Rican independence received support in exchange for Cuba's support for access to seaports by the landlocked countries and for the commodity producers' schemes for price stability.[27]

Above all, the times were fortuitous. The OPEC embargo had thrown the West onto the defensive and had given the Third World its chance, which it was not slow to seize. On January 30, 1974, Algerian President Houari Boumedienne, acting as chairman of the Non-Aligned Coordinating Bureau, wrote to UN Secretary-General Kurt Waldheim requesting that the United Nations call a special session of the General Assembly to consider raw materials problems of all types, not just oil. Nor was Waldheim dilatory in replying. On February 25, he advised UN members that a Sixth Special Session would be held on April 9, with the object of "securing optimum use of the world's natural resources for better conditions of social justice throughout the world."[28] Thanks to Algerian drive and staff work, the Non-Aligned provided the UN Secretariat with the agenda, back-up papers, and draft resolutions that the UN Sixth Special Session used as the basis for negotiations with the individual states.[29] It was a stunning performance, and a diplomatic triumph.

The momentum carried on through the rest of the year. In August 1974, the UN Conference on Population in Bucharest was turned into political theater, another platform for belaboring the West: Overpopulation was a Western red herring; what countries needed was not contraception but development; development was itself the best contraceptive. In November, the World Food Conference convened in Rome, and it provided another platform for denunciation of the West in general and of the United States in particular. In December, the Twenty-ninth General Assembly adopted the Charter of Economic Rights and Duties of States (CERDS), which complemented the NIEO by setting out principles and guidelines to govern international economic behavior. The developed countries found the charter repugnant and voted against it, but they were outvoted by the Third World majority.

In the United States, regard for the United Nations, never high in the best of times, fell to a new low, and the United States cut its share of assessed contributions to the United Nations from 33 percent to 25 percent. Resentment toward the Third World was intense and produced an ideological backlash from leading writers and academics, a hostile reaction from Congress, and a policy of defense in the administration rather than an imaginative response. Moreover, the Third World demands came at a bad time for the United States. The president was increasingly preoccupied with Watergate, and the country was increasingly preoccupied with the president. Nixon's resignation in August 1974, the installation of a new president, and the cleaning up of the mess took center stage. It was no time for a reevaluation of U.S. policy in the United Nations, let alone for laying the cornerstone of a New International Economic Order. The administration could not have done anything if it had wanted to. In his speech to the Twenty-ninth General Assembly, President Gerald Ford warned against the "tyranny of the majority," and at the end of the session UN Ambassador John Scali did the same.

Recapitulation

By the end of 1974, the world system had gone through a demoralizing series of shocks: the monetary crisis and abandonment of the Bretton Woods system without anything to take its place; a food crisis, which although abating showed how fragile a matter world food security is; and the oil crisis, which affected both industrialized and developing countries profoundly and imposed an enormous new demand on the already strained monetary balance, revealing, once again, the vulnerability of an interdependent world. The cumulative effect was an ominous world recession, mounting inflation, and increasing unemployment — the beginning of what seemed to be an erosion of all the gains made during the previous two decades.

Added to those problems were grave doubts about the social and economic system itself. The Stockholm conference on the environment in 1972 had alerted the world to the growing, and possibly irreversible, damage to the environment, and in the same year the Club of Rome had published a study asserting that the world had almost reached its "limits to growth." But population growth continued its geometric rate of increase, and the demands on resources, both by developed and by developing nations, continued to expand. The world seemed to be running out of control and doomsday predictions proliferated.

Something irremedial had happened to the postwar consensus. The world found itself locked in a heated debate about equity, cooperation, and authority; about growth and conservation, development, money, food, and resources. The world order itself was being called to account, but there was nothing to replace it. Everything was top priority. Europe and the United States were in conflict over oil. The OPEC nations suddenly carried all the high cards. The Third World had flung down the gauntlet. The West was again "at bay," but this time from the South.

The United States in particular was passing through a bad period, increasingly withdrawn and indecisive. During the Watergate months, it had slumped to its nadir of prestige and self-respect, angry at the world and isolated in its anger. In spite of Kissinger's admonition to put Vietnam behind them, the American people lived with a gnawing sense of guilt that the United States had "failed" in Vietnam. Nixon's resignation had provided some grim satisfaction that the "system" had worked—worked well enough to expel a man who had brought disgrace to his office and to replace him with a "decent" successor. Nevertheless, U.S. relations internationally were in serious trouble. The wave of hostility from the Third World marked a serious breakdown in U.S. relations with the developing countries as a whole; the fact that Americans neither understood nor sympathized with Third World attitudes and problems was beside the point. Overshadowing everything was the economic situation; the very idea of an open, free-market international economic system was suddenly and obviously at risk because of monetary instability, oil price rises, and challenges by the Third World.

The only area that did not seem to be at risk was national defense or collective security. There was no apparent threat to the Western alliance, inward or outward. The early seventies were the years of détente: West Germany and the USSR reached agreement on Berlin; the NATO foreign ministers agreed to the European Security Conference and to engage in mutual and balanced force reduction (MBFR) talks; Nixon signed the antiballistic missile (ABM) treaty in Moscow; and Leonid Brezhnev accepted the Common Market.

But the sense of security was deceptive. At the very time the United States was withdrawing from Asia, the Cold War was shifting to the Third World, its manifestations just over the horizon. Within a year, the world would see the fall of South Vietnam and of Cambodia to Communist forces. In Southern Africa, independence for Mozambique and Angola would bring in Marxist regimes, would lead to the introduction of Cuban expeditionary forces and to additional Soviet military aid. What the United States still had to recognize was the apparent contradiction between détente in the West and continuing Soviet support for national liberation movements in the Third World.[30]

The early seventies were years of extraordinary change and uncertainty, a time when the great issues of the next quarter century were being introduced on the agendas of the world's governments. Secretary Kissinger, reflecting on the chastening experience of the previous year, said in a television interview on January 16, 1975:

> One central fact of our period is that more than a hundred nations have come into being . . . and they too [along with the five major centers] must be central participants in this [international] process. So that for the first time in history

foreign policy has become truly global . . . I feel we are at a watershed. We're at a period of extraordinary creativity or a period when really the international order came apart politically, economically and morally. I believe that with all the dislocation we now experience there also exists an extraordinary opportunity to form, for the first time in history, a truly global society carried by the principle of interdependence. And if we act wisely and with vision, I think we can look back to the turmoil as the birth pangs of a more creative and better system. If we miss the opportunity, I think there is going to be chaos.[31]

Those were not empty sentiments. During the next few months, the United States tried to break out of its malaise, to get a grip on itself, to resume a constructive place in international society, and to reinforce actively what it conceived to be its basic interest in the world.

The North-South Dialogue: Phase 1

For the Third World, the diplomatic offensive was just the beginning. Encouraged by the 1974 victories at the Sixth Special Session and the Twenty-ninth General Assembly, Third World countries had been hard at work putting together a unified front with the OPEC states to make it clear that they would not negotiate on energy unless the northern states reviewed other raw materials problems as well. The Twenty-ninth General Assembly was followed immediately by Third World meetings in February in Dakar and Algiers on raw materials policy and the possibility of OPEC financing for other LDC producer cartels. The meetings were also called to reach consensus on concrete proposals for transforming the NIEO from rhetoric to reality through specific reforms of the rules and norms of the existing international system. Most of these proposals were subsequently incorporated into the Lima Declaration adopted at the Second General Conference of the UN Industrial Development Organization (UNIDO) in Lima, Peru, in March 1975.[1]

From Confrontation to Negotiation

The United States cast the sole negative vote against the Lima Declaration, with Belgium, Canada, the Federal Republic of Germany, Israel, Italy, Japan, and the United Kingdom abstaining. U.S. Chief Delegate W. Tapley Bennett, Jr., reported "that since the USG had not changed its position on the Declaration and Program of Action for a NIEO and had only recently started a review of policy in preparation for the 7th Special Session, the U.S. delegation at Lima was charged essentially with a holding action."[2] Bennett's observations on the other delegations are revealing. The G-77, he reported, maintained solidarity. Complaints of the moderates, mainly Asian, about radical elements of the G-77 in no way affected the moderates' voting. Group B, on the other hand, "tended to splinter."

Group B attitudes spanned the Third World leanings of the Netherlands, the "progressive" position of the Scandinavian delegations and Australia, the desire of the French to appear forthcoming to the LDCs, the skittishness of the Swiss about too close an association with hard-line U.S. positions, concern of the UK, FRG and Japan regarding Lima's effect on preparations for the 7th Special Session and the vigorous defense of the U.S. of its own position.[3]

Another sign of the way the wind was blowing was the fact that on February 28, 1975, the European Community (EC) had signed the Lomé Convention with the forty-six African, Caribbean, and Pacific (ACP) countries, providing joint institutions for EC-ACP commercial, industrial, and financial cooperation.

The United States had, however, come around to accepting the idea of negotiations with OPEC, and the two sides finally met in April 1975 in Paris to prepare for a full-scale energy conference in September. But the meeting was quickly deadlocked, and it dissolved in failure because the industrialized nations — in agreement for a change — refused to give equal priority to the broader issues of development.[4] The Paris meeting was not an utter loss, however. It proved to the West that OPEC and the other LDCs would hang together no matter what. There was no alternative, therefore; the West would have to talk about development, finance, and commodities if it wanted to talk about oil.

Clearly, a new policy was needed. Thomas O. Enders, who was then assistant secretary of state for economic affairs and in charge of the oil negotiations has recalled:

> The change of the U.S. policy from the rather unprofitable one of confrontation to cooperation toward the Third World resulted from a number of elements and concerns during the months previous to the Seventh Special Session. But it was very much at Kissinger's initiative. He felt that we had to tell the Third World that we had heard them and were concerned.
>
> As to what prompted Kissinger's concern, I would say that it was partly due to the failure of the Paris talks, where we had gone to talk oil but found that we would have to talk development, commodities, and finance as well and that the OPEC countries would not discuss one without the other.
>
> Then there was the feeling that we could not repeat the experience of the Sixth Special Session. We had to free ourselves from earlier constraints (U.S. Treasury) and reassert traditional U.S. leadership.
>
> There was also strong interest among liberals in Congress from both parties — viz., Senators Percy, Javits, Mondale — who had formed a joint Senate-House group and were trying to push the administration and the State Department to go faster. They were alarmed by the LDC backlash and the consequence of further oil price increases. Kissinger and Ford wanted to respond

to this interest, not to seem insensitive to the party liberals.[5]

Meanwhile, other long-range concerns gradually made themselves felt. There was a rising awareness of Third World trade as a percentage of the gross national product (GNP), growing U.S. reliance on imported raw materials, increased LDC bargaining strength vis-à-vis multinational corporations, and the question of LDC markets for U.S. exports and investment. Politically, the United States was depending more on cooperation to manage global problems through multilateral negotiations (Law of the Sea, nuclear proliferation, environment, food, etc.). Furthermore, as U.S. influence declined, the United States needed increased cooperation from its industrial partners.[6]

The result was a major policy review during the spring and summer of 1975, led by senior officials of the State Department with Assistant Secretary Enders in charge. Heretofore, planning had been under the State Department's Bureau of International Organization Affairs (IO), which is normally responsible for UN affairs within the State Department. That bureau had begun to prepare for the Seventh Special Session the day the Twenty-ninth General Assembly closed down, but Kissinger had ignored it.

> Good men had been at work, from the Bureau, from the Agency for International Development, from Policy Planning, but none of them controlled resources, least of all those directly responsible for UN affairs. Enders did. He was in charge of the international economic policy of the world's largest economy. He could give and take within that economy and between it and other economies.[7]

Putting the major policy review under Enders's direction was more important than mere bureaucratic rivalry, as that action effectively assigned, henceforth, responsibility for policy and negotiation on North-South issues to the particular bureau of the Department of State that was primarily responsible for the support of U.S. business and the maintenance of the open, free-market world economy. The change was the logical thing to do since the NIEO is anti–free market in general and anti–U.S. business in particular. On the other hand, the new assignment meant that Third World relations — heretofore an ill-defined mixture of political, economic, and development considerations — would clearly be subordinated to economic imperatives. From this point on, conflict was inevitable.

On July 14, in a speech to the Wisconsin Institute of World Affairs in Milwaukee, Secretary Kissinger laid out the new line — tough and realistic but cooperative.[8] He talked of a new global environment, of a world with many centers of power, of ideological differences, of the struggle for economic security. The central focus of U.S. foreign policy, he said, is to help shape a new international structure based on equilibrium rather than on confrontation.

But, according to Kissinger, the United Nations had been turning from a forum for accommodation into a setting for confrontation. He cited "destruction of its moral influence," "imposition of increasingly arbitrary will," "ideological confrontation," and "bloc voting, loaded voting and biased results" as some of the principal evils.

The United States, he said, believes in a cooperative approach. "We have heard and have begun to understand your concerns." The United States is prepared to be responsive to what works and to assist internal efforts of LDCs to help themselves. The challenge, he observed, is basically political, but the LDCs cannot expect the United States to make political decisions with no thought for their economic consequences.

Buried within Kissinger's speech was a veiled threat. The United States will help and will cooperate, but the LDCs must stop their nonsense. They are destroying the United Nations, he alleged, and the United States has the option to pull out. Confrontation tactics can be a two-edged sword.

The Seventh Special Session of the UNGA

The Seventh Special Session held in September 1975 met for ten days and covered six items, as defined by the Economic and Social Council (ECOSOC) at its fifty-ninth session: international trade, transfer of resources and monetary reform, science and technology, industrialization, agricultural development, and restructuring the UN system. Algerian Foreign Minister Bouteflika set the stage in his keynote speech. He recalled the Sixth Special Session and reiterated the demands made then for the establishment of the NIEO. It had become clear, he said, that the prosperity of the West is derived to a large extent from the draining of the wealth and the exploitation of the peoples of the Third World. The Seventh Special Session presented the delegates with historic possibilities, and he called on "the more fortunate to yield to the legitimate aspirations of those to whom history and sometimes nature have been ungenerous."[9]

Nevertheless, the Seventh Special Session opened on a note of conciliation, the result of months of informal preparation around the world since the sixth session. The position of the European countries had already been subjected to some modification during the negotiation of the Lomé Convention in February and at the Commonwealth meeting of heads of governments in Kingston, Jamaica, in May 1975. But the U.S. position was a major turnabout, marking the end to almost two years of U.S. stonewalling.[10]

Kissinger's speech (which in his absence was delivered by Ambassador Moynihan) picked up the forthright Milwaukee theme.[11] We can respond with common sense and vision to the problem of improving the conditions of mankind, he said, or we can let the opportunity slip away. The United States is committed to constructive effort and to practical action, but nations have to reconcile their competing goals — LDC claims for a just share of the global prosperity and a greater role in their own economic destiny, developed country (DC) claims for reliable supplies of energy and raw materials at fair prices. Cooperation is necessary as the goals cannot be reached in isolation. Therefore, countries must go beyond obsolete nineteenth-century economic dictums, strident nationalism, bloc politics, useless rhetoric, and sterile debate and get down to business.

The bulk of the speech consisted of a wide variety of proposals and commitments in every substantive area: assuring economic security, accelerated growth, trade, commodities, and aid to the least developed countries (LDCs). The speech contained more than can be summarized here: suffice to say, it had something for everyone, but it was, nonetheless, realistic and provided the basic statement of U.S. policy in each sector. It is doubtful if any single government has ever before promised so much at one time to so many.

Finally, Kissinger lectured the special session delegates on the mechanism for getting results. No country or group of countries, he said, should have exclusive power in areas basic to the welfare of others (such as OPEC). Countries should seek to establish real communities of economic interest, not just arbitrary blocs or artificial majorities. These communities must be more representative as LDCs emerge as economic powers, and conference participation should be limited to the parties directly involved.

The main impact of the speech was the perceived willingness on the part of the United States to recognize the legitimacy of the southern demand for serious negotiations and to begin that process in a series of different venues.[12] The speech was well received. UK Ambassador Ivor Richards pronounced it "the most significant American speech on economic policy since the Marshall Plan," and press reaction around the world was overwhelmingly favorable, although there were some sour notes from the left-wing and OPEC countries, which Kissinger had criticized.[13]

This time the United States had Congress behind it in principle, but would the new policy work? That depends, said Senator Jacob Javits at a reception following the speech, on what happens. "If the Special Session degenerates into vituperation and obstruction," he said, "it will be an opportunity lost. It is now up to the developing countries."[14]

Observers have been at pains to emphasize the positive influence the U.S. "turnabout" had on the Third World.

> The willingness of the United States to include the developing world on its
> 1975–76 diplomatic agenda was all that was needed to elicit a constructive
> response from the world's developing countries. . . . The Group of 77 ac-
> cepted the Kissinger speech . . . as signalling a willingness to negotiate,
> worked hard to produce a compromise resolution . . . and ultimately sup-
> ported a final draft which considerably diluted their earlier demands.[15]

There is some truth in that view, but the actuality is more interesting. Ambassador Enders has stated that the final success of the Seventh Special Session was due very much to Ambassador Moynihan. Despite Moynihan's
reputation for being "in opposition," he wanted to turn to cooperation.
With the Seventh Special Session getting nowhere, he made a cut-and-
paste job of competing DC and LDC resolutions as a first draft of a compromise resolution. Moynihan then gave the draft to Enders to get the administration's acceptance. According to Enders, he got Kissinger's OK and
even Bill Simon's (Treasury Secretary), who disagreed with everything in it
but finally "went along." Enders spent about two weeks of twenty-hour
days working on the thing.[16]

Moynihan himself has provided a fascinating step-by-step account of the
efforts to work out the compromise in the United Nations. Kissinger and
Mexico's foreign minister, Emilio Rabasa, had decided that they had to do
something or the Seventh Special Session would be a failure. They thus got
their respective ambassadors (Moynihan and Alfonso Garcia Robles)
together and told them that it was up to them, the two of them were to work
together and get the job done. After working nonstop for several days and
all night Saturday, agreement on the compromise draft was reached at last.
But shortly after noon on Sunday, at the NBC studio where Moynihan was
to appear on "Meet the Press," he learned that Bouteflika had rejected the
agreement. There was one day—Monday—left before the end of the session. Moynihan told the press that the United States was disappointed but
that the rejection "wouldn't cost *us* anything at all." In any case, he said, the
United States was through negotiating. Nevertheless, negotiations continued, and at 5 A.M. Tuesday, just a few hours before the opening of the
General Assembly, the special session reached agreement.[17]

The delegates were impressed. The delegate from Mauritania declared,
"It was unlike any other debate in the General Assembly in that this one
had been a genuine conversation amongst nations. New ideas have been introduced and expanded upon, delegations have listened to each other in
earnest dialogue." Jan Pronk, the Dutch chairman of the main negotiating
committee, said, "Because of the political atmosphere in which consensus
had been reached, the Special Session was quite an important happening."
Moynihan, himself, announced that "Perhaps never in the history of the

United Nations has there been so intensive and genuine a negotiation among so many nations on so profoundly important a range of issues."[18]

The delegates' comments are self-congratulatory but forgivable. To evaluate the Seventh Special Session, one should remember the events of the previous two years, the atmosphere of crisis, the fact that the world economy was still in the midst of groping its way through recession into stagflation, that the Third World had lined up solidly against the United States, and that the United States itself had had to fight off a mood of resentment and withdrawal and to come to grips with realities, however disagreeable. To the men who had lived through that process, the achievement of a positive result from the Seventh Special Session seemed like a victory for common sense and compromise.[19]

The Paris Conference on
International Economic Cooperation (CIEC)

The year 1976 surely marked the height of the negotiating and organizing efforts concerning global economic and social issues. The recommendations of the World Food Conference of November 1974 were being further negotiated in meetings of the new World Food Council, and the Tokyo Round of international trade negotiations under the General Agreement on Tariffs and Trade (GATT) was well under way, having begun officially in February 1974. Separate and continuing negotiations on world monetary problems were conducted by the International Monetary Fund (IMF) and the World Bank (IBRD), and the recommendations of the Seventh Special Session were being carried out in a variety of agencies and subsidiary negotiations. World conferences — similar to those on environment, food, and population — were held on habitat, in Vancouver in May and June, and on world employment, in Geneva in June. The Third Conference on the Law of the Sea started in Caracas in March. In February, ministers of the G-77 met in Manila to draft a negotiating position for UNCTAD IV, which convened in May in Nairobi. The Non-Aligned convened its fifth summit in Colombo in August, and Western leaders held their economic summit in Puerto Rico. And, beginning in December 1975 and running through 1976, the Conference on International Economic Cooperation (CIEC) met in Paris.

The CIEC negotiations held center stage, so that the focus of attention on the NIEO moved directly from the Seventh Special Session in September 1975 to the Second CIEC Preparatory Meeting in October, which set the terms of reference for the full-scale conference to begin with a ministerial meeting in Paris in December. The CIEC was a unique conference since it covered, for the first time in history, multilateral negotiations on oil be-

tween consumer and producer nations as well as the monetary, trade, and development interests of the rest of the developing nations. Another significant fact was that the CIEC, hosted by the government of France, shifted the North-South dialogue out of the United Nations.

The structure of the conference reflected an earnest, business-like attitude. Instead of being another vast forum, CIEC participation was kept to a minimum consistent with fair representation. There were representatives from eight DC countries, including a single representative for the EC, and nineteen LDCs, including both OPEC and non-OPEC LDCs. It was hoped that this combination would provide balance within a group small enough to do business.[20] The OECD countries hoped, naively as it turned out, that the separation of OPEC and non-OPEC countries would minimize the chances for a repetition of Third World bloc tactics.

I shall make no attempt to review or even to summarize briefly the negotiations of the CIEC because they were too complex and too drawn out, but the objectives are easy to define. The North wanted assured supplies of oil, a producer-consumer agency to manage oil, and protection against arbitrary price increases. The OPEC countries wanted indexation of oil prices, Western commitments to energy conservation, and concessions to the non-oil-exporting LDCs. The non-oil-exporting LDCs wanted improvements in the prices of raw material exports, price stabilization, increased aid, and nonreciprocal trade preferences as well as other items on a long LDC list of demands.

The results of the CIEC were negligible: a DC commitment to work on a Common Fund and a new $1-billion Special Action Program for low-income countries. In the early hours of June 3, 1977, the conference came to a battered and confused end, and the eighteen-month "dialogue" between the North and the South, which had begun with so much enthusiasm and great hope in Paris, finished on a faint and joyless note. A hastily drafted and uncommonly bland report was presented for adoption to a glum and an exhausted audience at the conference's last plenary meeting.[21]

What went wrong? There are several answers. Control of oil was a very high card in the deck, and the West held nothing higher; it could not outbid OPEC. The West would not agree to indexation, and the few concessions it did make in other sectors were, by comparison, insignificant. And the West's hope that the "trilateral" organization of the conference might force OPEC's hand proved to be vain.

The West's highest card was the old economic order, which it was unlikely to give up for anything less than the major objective of a producer-consumer agency. Neither side was prepared or able to rise above its own special interests to see any validity in the other's views, let alone to see a common advantage.

Each side, especially the LDCs, miscalculated its own power. The LDCs relied inordinately on concepts of moral superiority and on the supposed guilt of the West. Recession and inflation were already eroding the LDC gains of 1973, and the oil exporters actually wanted to save the "oil card" for possible use in Middle East conflict bargaining. The DCs were divided on almost every item of the agenda between hardliners such as the United States and West Germany and countries such as the Netherlands that were more disposed to "cooperate." The EC was unable to adopt a line above the lowest common denominator.

The problems of the CIEC were too complex to be dealt with in such a short time. Relationships among economic and monetary issues, finance and energy, and commodity trade are close, and a change in one necessitates changes in others.[22] The negotiations suffered from mutual mistrust. The OECD countries were opposed to indexation for more than technical reasons, and they did not trust the oil producers to deliver the quid pro quo of a producer-consumer agency. The LDCs were never convinced of the sincerity of the West. The case-by-case approach to debt relief and commodities was seen as a device to divide the LDCs. The West felt that any loosening of solidarity might give the LDCs the opportunity to exercise the "tyranny of the majority."

The timing of the conference was unfortunate. The West was in the middle of a damaging recession, and from January to June 1976 there were four impending national elections—in Germany, Japan, Italy, and the United States. Neither side came to grips with fundamentals. The LDCs never showed much comprehension of what the NIEO would be, and the DCs defended the old order without question. The theme of interdependence figured prominently, but its real dimensions were unappreciated.[23] This list of problems is not an exhaustive one, but it is illustrative of some of the basic problems of the whole North-South dialogue.

But the CIEC was a case of the blind leading the blind. Neither North nor South could (or wanted to) see each other's point of view, and neither could envision a common ground. From the two extreme positions there was nowhere to go, no path to follow, no one to lead. The conference demonstrated, above all, that the sense of agreement and cooperation reached at the Seventh Special Session was superficial. What had been negotiated there were words not substance.

UNCTAD IV

While CIEC delegates were meeting in Paris, UNCTAD convened its fourth conference in Nairobi on May 5, 1976. That conference was and has been overshadowed by the CIEC, but UNCTAD IV is the functional link with the

Seventh Special Session, providing the continuity between it and subsequent work on the NIEO. The CIEC was really about oil, with side bets on finance, commodities, and trade. At UNCTAD IV those side bets were the main stakes. Furthermore, the Nairobi meeting carried on the spirit of the Seventh Special Session—a sense of hope, opportunity, and cooperation. Disillusion had not yet set in. In the opening speeches, UN Secretary-General Waldheim stressed that "political independence does not end the struggle . . . the achievement of economic decolonization and the creation of a NIEO" must be achieved. UNCTAD Secretary-General Gamani Corea evoked the poverty and degradation of millions of people in the Third World, and President Ferdinand Marcos of the Philippines predicted a bloody confrontation if the gap between reality and expectation was not closed.[24]

The agenda was relatively short, consisting of eight items that constituted the core concepts of the NIEO or the North-South dialogue: commodity trade; trade in manufactures and semimanufactures; transfer of technology; financial matters; cooperation among LDCs; trade with East Europe; special measures for the least developed, landlocked, and island nations; and UNCTAD institutional matters. The format was somewhat changed from that of the Seventh Special Session—commodities had been moved to the top, agricultural development had been deleted, and special measures for the disadvantaged countries and trade with the eastern bloc countries had been added. The Seventh Special Session had looked at the issues "once over lightly"; UNCTAD IV considered them a second time.

The United States went to UNCTAD IV in force, with a strong delegation that included eight congressmen and was headed by Secretary Kissinger and his deputy, Charles W. Robinson. Kissinger called on the conference to build on the accomplishments of the Seventh Special Session, continue the cooperative spirit, and accelerate its efforts. The time was one of opportunity, he said; with the world just emerging from severe recession, it was a decisive moment to "reinvigorate and improve the world's economic system." Carrying on with the spirit of his speeches in Milwaukee and to the Seventh Special Session, he warned delegates to get down to business and not to let the moment slip away in rhetorical attacks and peremptory demands.[25]

The U.S. program was forthcoming and positive and included another long inventory of offers and proposals. However, compared to the Seventh Special Session, the U.S. proposals were more specific and in a different order of priority, reflecting experience gained and new perspectives. The proposals covered commodities first, with a proposal for an international resources bank; technology transfer, including the establishment of an international industrialization institute and an international energy institute;

debt and balance-of-payments matters; and the needs of the poorest countries.[26]

Negotiations were mainly between the G-77 Manila Declaration, drawn up in January and February by the G-77 ministers as their negotiating paper, and the U.S.-prepared resolutions, based on the U.S. proposals that formed the basis of the DC position. The negotiations were arduous and continued through a "tumultuous" night after the official close of the meeting, but in the end they resulted in more than a dozen resolutions that provided the authority for a work program in UNCTAD and elsewhere until the next conference.[27]

The U.S. delegation chairman, Paul H. Boeker, called the conference "relatively successful" and declared that it had "maintained the atmosphere of constructive North-South dialogue launched at the 7th Special Session."[28] Most LDCs, he reported, found the offers of economic cooperation of sufficient interest to make a return to political confrontation unprofitable, and they worked toward compromise on most issues. The LDCs did not present the Manila Declaration as the only basis of discussion but proceeded on the basis of both sides' proposals. The top priority of the conference, as well as its major result, was an omnibus resolution on commodities that provided for commodity-by-commodity discussions between producers and consumers leading to actual commodity negotiations. The conference also initiated a series of meetings to examine a proposal for a Common Fund to finance buffer stocks, after which the UNCTAD secretary-general was to convene a negotiating conference no later than March 1977.

Boeker also cited some difficulties.[29] UNCTAD, he said, proved a difficult forum in which to reach agreement on complex development issues because of "intra-group coordination problems." Very little was achieved beyond the discussion on commodities and the resolution on the transfer of technology; concentration on the Common Fund "probably led to the sacrifice of . . . accomplishment in other areas." Even that work was slowed down by OPEC's refusal to contribute to a Common Fund through the OPEC Special Fund. Regional and personal rivalries frustrated efforts to establish a leadership group in the G-77, and positions taken by formal G-77 coordinators were sometimes disowned by regional groups or individual LDCs, which resulted in the overall impression of the G-77 being immobile. Coordination among Group B members also proved difficult, mainly because of the difficulty of reaching common European positions.

UNCTAD Secretary-General Corea called the negotiations a "watershed in the evolution of international policy,"[30] which was the appropriate thing for the UNCTAD secretary-general to say. Nevertheless, appearances — and there is good reason to believe that appearances were the last resort of negotiations that otherwise failed — were misleading, as subsequent events amply proved.

The Common Fund Negotiations

The Common Fund is an integral component of the UNCTAD-developed Integrated Programme for Commodities (IPC), and it was designed to help LDCs with problems associated with the commodity trade. LDCs are heavily dependent on commodity exports, sometimes on a single product, and so they are at the mercy of the notoriously unstable commodity market in which wide fluctuations in demand and price seriously affect LDCs' earnings, balance of payments, and development planning. The primary aim of the IPC, therefore, is to achieve stable conditions, including avoidance of excessive price fluctuations, as well as increased income, improved market access, economic diversification, and the expansion of processing in LDCs and LDC marketing facilities. Measures proposed included the negotiation of producer-consumer agreements on eighteen commodities, with priority given to ten "core" commodities of particular importance and the negotiation of a Common Fund. The Common Fund would be an independent $6-billion agency or bank designed to stabilize prices through the financing of buffer stocks.

Following UNCTAD IV and the CIEC, the Common Fund became the "centerpiece" of the NIEO. It came to embody the life and hope and principle of the NIEO,[31] but it was a forlorn hope at best, for the DCs were solidly opposed and had stonewalled their way through both UNCTAD IV and the CIEC. UNCTAD IV had established a timetable for preparatory meetings and for a negotiating conference on the establishment of a Common Fund, but the United States made it plain in its statement at the close of the conference that it had made no commitment and, although it would join preparatory meetings, it had serious doubts about the whole idea.[32]

The Common Fund proposal survived the CIEC, but just barely and as a cosmetic alternative to having the CIEC break up with no result. In March 1977, the European Council, meeting in Rome, had agreed in principle to the establishment of the Common Fund. That agreement had been confirmed at the London Summit in June, following which the CIEC agreed in principle on the establishment of a Common Fund. Its purposes, objectives, and other constitutional elements were to be further negotiated through UNCTAD.[33] As the language implies, the group of eight DCs had not accepted the UNCTAD conception of a Common Fund. By the same token, the group of nineteen LDCs had not abandoned it.[34]

Negotiations had been resumed in March 1977 in a one-hundred-nation conference in Geneva, but no agreement was reached. A second session was convened in November and a third and a fourth in 1978, but they too failed to reach substantial agreement. Again, in an attempt to avoid the appearance of total breakdown, the conference asked UNCTAD Secretary-

General Corea to reconvene the conference one last time before UNCTAD V in May 1979.

The closing weeks of 1978 were the low point for Third World negotiators, and they were marked by bitterness and anger. As reported by the *Guardian* Geneva correspondent, Iain Guest: "Another major casualty of the Common Fund saga is the 'new international economic order.' In balmier days UNCTAD officials talked of the common fund being the 'cutting edge of the new order.' Now, if it emerges at all, it will be as the result of a 'major concession' by the West, after a process of pulling teeth."[35] UNCTAD officials talked bleakly of a "disastrous impasse." Their apprehension was that failure to negotiate a Common Fund now would sabotage UNCTAD V and turn it into an "angry and retrospective debate."[36]

The trouble was mainly over the fund's role and size. During the three years of negotiations, Third World negotiators began to realize that there were commodity problems besides price fluctuations. Equally troublesome were single-commodity economies, low productivity, and commodities such as bananas that could not be stockpiled. The Third World concept of the Common Fund therefore began to expand to include a "second window" for financing economic diversification, improved production, and marketing systems. The DCs, opposed from the very beginning to the idea of the Common Fund but brought to reluctantly accept it, now opposed the fund's expansion into areas that, it was thought, would duplicate the role of the World Bank. The DCs were also bitterly opposed to the size of the fund, $6 billion, on the grounds, among other things, that a fund of that size would put control of the commodity trade into the hands of the producer countries.

The November 1978 meeting was terminated at the request of the G-77 on the grounds that the main problem was not technical but political and that the DCs' attitude was in clear contradiction to the commitments made at the CIEC.[37] The Group B representatives voiced "regret," felt that real progress could be made, and asserted that there had been a broadening of consensus. U.S. negotiator E. Allan Wendt said that the problem was basically one of different approaches.

> The LDCs wanted governments to commit themselves in principle to the creation and financing of a common fund . . . they believed the details could be worked out later.
>
> We [Group B] wanted to explore exactly what the Common Fund would do, what measures it would undertake, the product it would be concerned with and the problems it would deal with. We felt it would be impossible for governments and finance ministers and central banks to consider any financial obligations to support such activities until there is some precise indication of these matters.[38]

The Common Fund was also the victim of a post-CIEC malaise, during which the momentum of the Seventh Special Session fell off. What went wrong? What had happened to the spirit of the Seventh Special Session, even of UNCTAD IV, and to the fine words and commitments? From the LDC side, the charges were hypocrisy, failure of political will, and indifference on the part of the North. According to Ambassador Enders: "A lot of people were turned off by LDC intransigence in CIEC. They felt that the U.S. had made honest offers and contributions but that these had produced no response from the Third World which refused to moderate even its most extreme demands."[39] There was obviously a lot more to the failure than that since there were different views within the administration, and there was a continuing willingness to negotiate, even if to no evident purpose. Perhaps the real question is not What were the obstacles to progress? but What was keeping the Common Fund alive? The rest is speculation until the history of the North-South dialogue has been written. In the meantime, we must content ourselves with these glimpses of what was apparent and what has been remembered and pass on to Phase 2 of the dialogue.

There was a long agenda of unfinished business left over from the Seventh Special Session and UNCTAD IV; in fact, most of the proposals remained to be implemented. But it was not merely unfinished business that characterized the next phase. For the Third World at least it was time to begin assessing past negotiations and future courses of action, a new effort that received its moral impetus at Arusha, Tanzania, in December 1978.

The Road to Manila

December 1978, Arusha, Tanzania: Third World leaders met for three days to review the status of the North-South dialogue. This was a meeting of the leaders in their private capacities, and they met because of their concern for "the gravity of the situation." The mood was one of hopelessness at getting the North to do anything substantial. But the situation was not completely hopeless, for, if there was no hope of significant cooperation from the North, there were always hitherto unexplored ways and means for the Third World to "go it alone."[1] The statement released to the press at the end of the meeting declared: "The North-South dialogue has moved from the era of declaration to the era of negotiation. There is urgent need for the South to adjust to the requirements and opportunities of the new situation which its collective efforts produced. The phase of petition is over. That of organized, practical action must begin."[2]

The maiden issue of the *Third World Quarterly,* published by the Third World Foundation in London, projected a grim outlook. Editor Altaf Gauhar wrote:

> 1979 could well determine the outcome of the North-South debate. Will the crumbs of "economic concession" gratify the Third World into abandoning the pursuit of a New International Economic Order? Will advocates of the present system yield to the necessity of its fundamental restructuring? . . . UNCTAD is due to meet. . . . All attempts to come to some substantive understanding on the Common Fund have been frustrated. The debt or burden of developing countries cannot be alleviated by niggardly gestures of charity toward the poorest of the poor. It will be a weary procession of Ministers treading toward a barren conclave in Manila.[3]

Commonwealth Secretary-General Shridath S. Ramphal, a "moderate," warned that without substantial improvement soon, "all hell will break loose" in the conference halls, and "disaster will overtake many countries," beginning "a serious international decline" both in the South and in the North.[4]

Reflected in the remarks is a sense of urgency that was largely lacking in the North. There is also a sense of impotence, neglect, and frustration over northern "indifference." "We had high hopes when Dick Cooper [U.S. undersecretary of state for economic affairs] joined the administration," said Ramphal, "but nothing changed. What happens to people when they get into office?"[5]

The International Wheat Agreement (IWA)

The year 1979 opened with negotiations on the renewal of the International Wheat Agreement (IWA), which confirmed the prevailing sense of pessimism rather than dispelling it. The food crisis of the early seventies had led to the November 1974 World Food Conference in Rome and to recommendations for urgent and sweeping international measures to meet the immediate and long-range problems of the world food supply. The key recommendation of the conference had been the creation of an international food reserve system that would provide security of supply and stability of world market prices. The eminently sensible recommendation received universal support, but governments were not so enthusiastic about its implementation, and improved harvests reduced the sense of urgency. Because the United States was the major supplier nation, the Saudi Arabia of grain, other governments waited to see what the United States would do. But within the U.S. government, policy differences prevented the adoption of any concrete proposals.

Since World War II, the United States had unilaterally provided the world's reserve stocks, bought and stored at the taxpayers' expense. When demand rose to meet supply during the early seventies, it was no longer necessary to stock surplus grains to maintain the market price, and the U.S. taxpayers, already pressed by higher food prices and stagflation, resented paying 100 percent of the cost of a world supply and stabilization system. Agriculture Secretary Butz was determined to get the Department of Agriculture "out of the grains business," so the efforts, mainly those of the State Department, to fulfill the commitments made at the World Food Conference fell on barren ground. They had to wait until the Carter administration, encouraged by falling prices and the need to provide support to the farmer, resumed the traditional policy that had been abandoned by the Republican administration under Nixon and Ford. However, in line with the recommendations of the World Food Conference, U.S. policy was that the burden of carrying world food stocks ought to be shared.

It was September 1977, therefore, before the United States submitted a formal proposal to the International Wheat Council (IWC) to set up a system of food reserve stocks.[6] The proposal called for, inter alia, wider international cooperation; changes in the basic framework of the IWA; rules and privileges that would apply equally to all participants, importers, and exporters; and more comprehensive food aid, at a world level of 10 million tons annually, with shared responsibility.

Six months later, in March 1978, the first seventy-nation UNCTAD conference was called to renegotiate the IWA. That conference failed, and a second one met in November 1978, but it also ended inconclusively with the recommendation that a third conference be held in early 1979. The problems were manifold. The United States and other exporters wanted the IWA separated from the multilateral trade negotiations (MTNs) so that a holdup in the MTNs would not affect the IWA. The EC and Japan refused to allow that separation unless they were compensated in the MTNs for a concession. The United States wanted a stock of 30 million tons; the EC refused to go above 15 million tons. The LDCs wanted a lower "trigger price" range, and the United States wanted a trigger price high enough to meet production costs. The LDCs wanted additional aid to build stocks, which the DCs opposed on the grounds that the IWA was not an aid scheme.[7]

The third conference convened on January 22, 1979, but it too ended in an impasse, mainly over the size of the stock and the minimum-maximum prices. At the very end, the United States and the EC came close to agreement when the United States agreed to a stock level of 25 million tons, but at that point, the LDCs refused to accept the trigger price. A food aid convention with a guaranteed level of 7.6 million tons was offered as a persuader but was rejected, and on February 9, the conference broke up for the last time.[8]

The international management of food therefore reverted to the *status quo ante bellum*. Since the current IWA was due to expire in June 1979, the IWC extended the agreement for the fifth time for an additional two-year period, calling on all interested governments to try to resolve their problems.[9] U.S. Agriculture Secretary Robert Bergland warned the EC that the United States would now pursue "a world wheat marketing agreement with major exporting and importing countries outside the IWA"—meaning, to the exclusion of the EC.[10] The president of the World Food Council, Arturo R. Tanco of the Philippines, appealed "on behalf of the hungry people of the world" for governments to resolve their differences to avoid a repetition of the disasters of 1972–1974.[11]

For some mysterious reason, the food issue is out of the mainstream of the NIEO proposal, but it provides an excellent example of the problems of translating glibly endorsed goals into workable international agreements and of expanding the logic of conventional economics and conventional national self-interest to fit a wider "common interest." No nation wants to assume increased costs and thereby give an advantage to its competitor.

The United States took three years to arrive at even an internal policy agreement based on shared international responsibility. The EC could see no advantage in joining a program that the United States had been carrying and probably would continue to carry by itself. The LDCs, with the most to gain, were unwilling to assume any costs or responsibilities whatsoever. And, if the United States favored a reserve system, it did not favor such a system in isolation but as part of a commodity agreement on grains. In short, the food problem demonstrates how an ultimate objective that is shared by all can be subverted to the pursuit of collateral objectives. President Tanco was fully justified in wringing his hands.

Fourth G-77 Ministerial Conference at Arusha

Ministers of the G-77 met for their fourth ministerial meeting prior to UNCTAD V in Arusha on February 12, 1979,

> to reaffirm our spirit of collective solidarity and collective self-reliance and to decide on a collective negotiating strategy for the Fifth session of the United Nations Conference on Trade and Development to be held at Manila in May 1979 as well as a programme of action on collective self-reliance and mutually beneficial co-operation among ourselves.[12]

President of Tanzania Julius Nyerere set the tone of the meeting in his opening address, in which he stressed Third World unity and collective self-reliance above ideology and moralizing. Exploitation and domination were "facts," he said, not a matter of morality unless they go on into the future. The purpose of coming together, therefore, was for a common cause, not ideology. The G-77, he observed, represents a full spectrum of governments—from socialist to fascist; some poor, some relatively rich—which tends to provoke divisions. Therefore, he urged, the ministers must strengthen their unity, speak with one voice, and ensure that no one country makes a bilateral deal. At the same time, the G-77 countries must cooperate among themselves to build trade and establish Third World multinational corporations, shipping lines, research and development, and financial institutions. The G-77 needs staffs of experts, full-time economists paid for by the G-77, to provide the LDCs with the support the DCs get from the OECD.[13] Nyerere was reiterating the message articulated by Ramphal and confirmed at the December 1978 meeting of Third World "wise men" at Arusha.

There is no need here to review the Framework for Negotiations as it is discussed in detail and at length in Chapter 4. Of possibly even greater importance was the Plan for Collective Self-Reliance, which carried through on the theme developed in December 1978 and by President Nyerere in his opening speech. That plan has been largely overlooked by governments and press, but it represented a new focus and, in a sense, a hardening of the Third World position.

The heart of the program for collective self-reliance was the Action Plan, which was designed to strengthen the capacity of LDCs to negotiate with DCs and to reduce LDC dependency. The plan itself would be part of the structural change toward a more "rational international division of labor" and a "more efficient use of world resources." The Action Plan recommended a global system of trade preferences among developing countries (GSTP); cooperation among state trading organizations (STOs); establishment of multinational enterprises (MNEs); strengthening of subregional, regional, and interregional economic integration and cooperation; cooperation in the transfer of technology; measures for the least developed, landlocked, and island LDCs; monetary and financial cooperation; creation of multinational production enterprises; and promotion of technical cooperation.

The plan also envisaged an elaborate organization and support system to put the plan into action. To be formed were secretariats on subregional, regional, and interregional levels; action committees to launch projects of common interest; an intersecretariat working group; a coordinating committee on multinational payments arrangements and monetary cooperation; and a financing facility aimed at trading among LDCs. The plan also envisaged that the expertise and institutional support for setting up the system would be supplied by UNCTAD. Finally, it recommended that any assistance given for these purposes should be in addition to rather than in lieu of assistance already extended to developing countries under other arrangements.

On the surface, the Action Plan appeared to be just what the Third World needed. However, it also had familiar aspects that were bound to raise Western opposition—a new echelon of committees and institutions totally dependent for their implementation on outside resources and an unbalanced catalog of DC obligations and LDC demands. Non-LDC members of UNCTAD have strongly opposed LDC attempts to use UNCTAD for exclusive Third World purposes, departing from the principle of universality. Further, many of the programs proposed appeared to be protectionist, or otherwise in restraint of trade, for the development of competitive industrial enterprise in agrobusiness, metals, and capital goods industries or for processing in fertilizers, rubber, pulp, paper, and petrochemicals. Powerful DC commercial and industrial interests would take a dim view of the use of taxpayers' money to underwrite the development of Third World competition—even food aid must respect "traditional" market shares. The Action Plan was all too reminiscent of the ill-starred Alliance for Progress of the sixties, in which the self-help principle was translated in practice into demands for massive resource transfers, a spirit of jealous noninterference, and, ultimately, minimum results. Finally, the plan directly or obliquely suggested a managed economic system. As President Nyerere said, "it will not happen through the workings of laissez-faire."[14]

Tanzanian Minister of Communication and Transport Amir Jamal in his closing address continued the theme introduced by President Nyerere. "Truly," Jamal said, "this final document is the product of many acts of solidarity on the part of many delegates." "There are forces in the industrialized countries, not so much of nationalism as of those which somehow want to preserve their own standards of consumption, no matter what the implications may be for the rest of the world." Their "voracious appetite for accelerating consumption" may lead to "conflicts and tensions taking an even uglier character than ever before." However, the "forces of reason and progress" could introduce a "mutually stabilizing global process" involving greater material progress for the developing countries and greater "restraint" by the industrialized countries.[15]

The Arusha Programme was a sizable and well-organized document backed up by strong and sincerely felt declarations from Third World leaders. It was surprisingly moderate — no "roasting" of the North, no undue moralizing. It attempted to be realistic and concentrated on the means to win goals, not on the moral justice of those goals. The preferred method of change was clearly negotiation and not confrontation. The ultimate objective was a "rational and more equitable use of the earth's resources."[16] It also had its weaknesses: Unity is the only real bargaining chip, without which LDCs see themselves as helpless victims; there are no new ideas, no alternatives proposed to a strategy admittedly already a failure; self-reliance is dependent on outside resources; domestic reforms are largely overlooked. The Arusha Programme was exhaustive, leaving nothing to the imagination, but it did not have any obvious priorities or focus.

The Common Fund Negotiations

UNCTAD Secretary-General Gamani Corea convened the Third Session of the UN Negotiating Conference on the Common Fund on March 12, 1979, and he stressed the need to reach agreement before UNCTAD V. He had tried, but without success, to persuade Group B countries to send delegations at the ministerial level,[17] but the auspices were still good. Much had happened since the failure of the second session in December, and it had happened rather quickly. By early January, Group B had reached agreement on the basic elements of the Common Fund. These included acceptance of a second window to be financed separately from the first and acceptance of direct government contributions to both windows under specific conditions, both sticking points at previous talks.[18] The G-77 had worked out a unified and coherent concept at Arusha, which "welcomed" the functional and financial association of International Commodity Agreements (ICAS) with the fund and would respect their autonomy.[19] Each position had been made available to the other side well in advance of the third session, providing time for evaluation and comparison. And each side recognized the prospect of a ruinous confrontation at UNCTAD V if agreement were not reached on the Common Fund beforehand. The U.S. delegation arrived with the statement, "We think that we have negotiated long enough and it is now time to buckle down and reach agreement at this session."[20]

Agreement was reached on a "framework." Negotiations lasted through the scheduled week, over the weekend, into Monday, and until 3 A.M. Tuesday. The U.S. ambassador and representative to the United Nations at Geneva observed that the negotiations were "a significant step forward," that there had been no confrontation or political rhetoric, and that the Common Fund would now no longer be a controversial issue at UNCTAD V.[21]

His attitude, more relief than joy, was mirrored in the comments of the press. "The UNCTAD plan brings no joy . . . it is the usual grudging compromise."[22] "Relief, skepticism, caution and sheer exhaustion" was the reaction.[23] "After three years of windy debates . . . the Common Fund . . . might start operations in a couple of years' time, . . . but the agreement should be seen more as a confirmation of pregnancy than an actual birth."[24]

But there was an agreement and a start. The agreement provided for a fund with two purposes. The first window would finance buffer stocks, and the second window would finance commodity development, including research and development (R&D), productivity, marketing, and diversification. Government contributions to the first window would amount to $400 million, and voluntary contributions to the second window, $350 million. Decisions would be by consensus, with voting shares divided 47 percent to the G-77, 42 percent to Group B, 8 percent to Group D (socialist bloc), and 3 percent to China. Secretary-General Corea was asked to convene a conference before the end of 1979 to adopt articles of agreement.[25] In a final reservation, the United States refused to accept the voting shares because, it said, the division did not reflect a "balance of interests."[26]

However, the fund, what was left of it, was an acceptable compromise on both sides. The Third World had finally established an entity at the heart of the NIEO and a fund close to its own ideas, with two windows and government contributions to both. The West had achieved a "minimum loss" agreement without Third World "domination," assured independence of the ICAS, and a fund of "manageable" proportions. Thus ended, for the time being at least, the long disputatious wrangle over the Common Fund. It is impossible to do justice to a subject of such complexity — so disliked by the United States but the darling of the Third World — and no one on either side yet knows whether anything of substance was actually accomplished.

U.S. Policy in a "New Era"

In the meantime, the United States had been carrying out a major policy review. As early as July 1978 there had once again been a decision in the State Department to pull the administration's North-South policy into one "understandable package," partly in recognition that in 1979–1980 the United States would face another series of highly political North-South meetings.[27] Moreover, by late 1978, a series of destabilizing world events made a major rethinking mandatory. In a surprising volte-face, China broke out of its thirty years of self-imposed isolation and sought economic cooperation with the West. The Soviet Union had become overtly interventionist in Africa and Southeast Asia, where Vietnam had just invaded Cambodia. Both developments threatened to put SALT II and détente at risk. In Afghanistan, the U.S. ambassador had been murdered, Central America was again in revolution, and in Iran the Ayatollah Ruhollah Khomeini had just toppled the shah in a stunning and popular revolution. Meanwhile, OPEC prices were edging up again, and the economic indicators showed alarming signs of a new recession. Uncertainty, tumult, and a sense of vulnerability produced carping among the Western allies, and accusations of weakness were directed at President Carter. It was a period of extraordinary complexity and of divided counsel among the allies and within the U.S. administration. A coherent policy line was needed. While the Third World met at Arusha to work out its own economic salvation, the United States tried again to get a grip on itself. The views of the two sides were as far apart as ever.

On February 20, 1979, President Carter spoke at the Georgia Institute of Technology on "America's Role in a Turbulent World."[28] Although asserting that the United States was still the leading power in "moving the world closer to a stable peace and genuine security," Carter acknowledged the substantial challenge of recent events — Iran, Cambodia, SALT II, the Middle East — and the widespread conditions of poverty throughout the Third World. "It is still a world of danger," he said, "a world in which democracy and freedom are still challenged, a world in which peace must be rewon day by day," and he called for the United States to continue to accept the challenge of leadership. If there was nothing substantially new in his speech, it did reflect the first, albeit tentative, attempt to reassert publicly America's role as a world leader.

Meanwhile, a North-South policy paper was being put together in the State Department. A meeting in Seattle, the Northwest Regional Conference on the Emerging International Order, was concentrating on Third World problems and seemed to provide the appropriate forum to get the maximum exposure before UNCTAD V.[29] On March 30, Secretary of State Cyrus Vance outlined the essentials of U.S. policy toward Third World development, providing the putative reply to the Arusha Programme.[30]

Vance's speech was a significant departure from Kissinger's approach at the Seventh Special Session and at UNCTAD IV. The "basket of goodies" approach was gone, replaced by a balanced and reasoned-out statement of interests and policies to serve those interests. As a basis, the United States sought to foster the growth of a global community, not a world "rigidly divided into Northern and Southern blocs," in which all would recognize common responsibilities, the rich would help the poor, international deliberations would be focused on serving human needs, and every nation would be dedicated to economic growth and justice. The distinction between North and South was eroding, Vance asserted. Much had already been accomplished, but much remained to be done to bring developing countries into the world trading system. The forthcoming North-South negotiations would be an opportunity, provided the delegates avoided "endless debate on sterile texts and focused instead on concrete development problems which *directly* affect people's lives" (italics mine). The United States, for its part, would concentrate on basic needs, energy, food, health, and technology. This policy was what the American people wanted and it had been approved by Congress.

In other words, Secretary Vance was saying that U.S. policy would be a continuation of its traditional bilateral policy of basic needs development and that the U.S. would cooperate in forthcoming negotiations on such matters. It is important to understand that the U.S. traditional development program and the NIEO are essentially separate concepts that bear little relation to each other, however badly they may be confused in argument. By implication, the United States was not interested in the "sterile debates" of the NIEO, hardly good news to the Third World. Mahmoud Mestiri, Tunisian ambassador to the United Nations and chairman of the G-77 who also spoke at the Seattle conference, retorted that the "Carter Administration does not really have a foreign policy for the Third World. It is just floating and trying to avoid confrontation."[31]

A month later, on May 1, Vance spoke in Chicago and gave a broad sketch of U.S. policy in an "era of change" again with an emphasis on the Third World.[32] It was an "important" speech and a complex statement — an attempt to make sense out of a period of rapid change, increasing complexity, incipient chaos, disorder, and uncertainty. Vance alchemized a mixture of Cold War realpolitik, Wilsonian idealism, and American buoyancy and optimism into a vision of progress, balance, security, stability, and moral good sense and attempted to integrate Third World and global interests into the traditional foreign policy framework of U.S. and allied economic, political, and strategic interests.

The speech was an affirmation of U.S. power, a promise of cooperation with traditional allies and China, a promise of cooperation with and assistance to developing countries, and a warning to the Soviets not to capitalize on Third World problems and disputes. The United States had nothing to fear from change, however widespread. The United States and the developed democracies had an unsurpassed ability to thrive in a world of change — indeed they were themselves the engines of change.

The statement affirmed America's continued dedication to self-determination, fundamental human rights, the right of popular change within nations, and an open, pluralistic international society. It rejected the use of military force in the Third World. The United States would, however, help to resolve regional disputes, oppose outsiders trying to exploit Third World conflicts for international purposes, and help Third World countries foster democracy and humane and indigenous governments and institutions, and assure national independence. The United States would help to bring the more advanced LDCs more fully into the international system and assist economic development through well-managed assistance programs.

The emphasis Vance gave to the Third World was generous, especially as it occurred in the context of U.S. economic, military, and political interests. In that sense, the statement represented an attempt to widen the traditional context of foreign policy interests, and perhaps it reflected Vance's reputed desire to concentrate on Third World affairs for the rest of his term of office, once the SALT II Treaty had been concluded and the debate for its ratification was over.[33]

What *New York Times* columnist James Reston called the "Quiet Voice of Vance" was, in effect, a "traditional" U.S. foreign policy speech with a difference. The ideals were there — freedom, democracy, the open economic order, collective security — but instead of the clarion call of JFK almost twenty years before, Vance declared that the United States was no longer responsible for the world, that it was now only one among several major powers. The use of U.S. military force in the Third World was ruled out. The internal affairs of other nations were their business. The U.S. interest was not in other nations becoming like the United States; it was that all nations be free of domination by others. What the United States could and would do was to help other nations develop their own institutions and strengthen their economic policies "which work in practical ways to advance freedom." The world system as a whole was pluralistic and demanded a diplomacy of cooperation. The world was moving into a "new era" in which the United States could not alone dictate events.

4
UNCTAD V:
A Case Study of Negotiations

The Monday following Vance's speech, May 7, 1979, delegates of 159 nations convened UNCTAD V in Manila to attempt, once again, to use the negotiating process to break the logjam of cross-purposes, to find a common ground, to avoid a zero-sum conclusion. They convened on the assumption that they could achieve those things if the right combination were discovered. No one had yet questioned the negotiating process in spite of the minimal gains previously achieved—or at least, no one had yet discovered a viable alternative. The reason for the lack of progress hitherto remained a mystery; there seemed no good reason for failure; each side was driven to blaming the other. In its report on the North-South problem, the Brandt Commission pondered the failure of UNCTAD V and asked, "Did the delegations of the South perhaps not concentrate enough on the vital issues of mutual interests? Or were countries of the North simply lacking in political will to make major concessions?"[1]

In this chapter, therefore, I shall take a detailed look at the negotiations themselves on the premise that the key to the puzzle may not be in the openly stated aims and objectives—on which there is actually much agreement on both sides—but, rather, in what happens at the negotiating table. Unless we know clearly what happens at the negotiating table, we cannot be sure we are dealing with reality. Even a cursory glance at the CIEC demonstrates the importance of the negotiating process per se as an integral component of the North-South dialogue and as a crucial, if little appreciated, factor in determining the outcome of the dialogue. The failure of the CIEC was largely due to the dynamics of the negotiations. The high cards were control of the oil supply on the one hand and control of the old international economic order on the other. Neither side was yet desperate enough to make a concession; neither side trusted the other to deliver the goods if concessions were made. Similarly, to understand fully U.S. policy toward the NIEO, one must look at the negotiating process itself, a crucial aspect of international relations that is seldom if ever mentioned in official announcements. The negotiations at UNCTAD V covered the central elements of the NIEO and provide, in effect, a case history of the entire subject.[2]

But first, a few words about the NIEO. It must be defined more precisely before proceeding further, for it has become all things to all men, a widening collection of problems and proposals for change and reform in every sector of economic life and beyond. It is easy to lose one's way amid the welter of declarations, conventions, plans, and programs, but, at heart, the NIEO is a rather straightforward and succinct idea that focuses on the central interlocking elements of world economic life, trade, finance, and development.[3]

The basic premise is that the old international economic order is out of date and does not reflect the needs of the modern world with over one hundred new nations struggling to develop. The old economic order, it is believed, has become a monopoly of the haves (the old industrialized nations), serves their needs, and keeps the new nations in perpetual dependence and, in many cases, perpetual poverty, inequality, and subordination. The gap between the developed and the developing countries is widening every year.

The NIEO seeks to change the situation, to redress the economic and political imbalances in a world in which 30 percent of the population enjoys 70 percent of the wealth. Under the new order, LDCs will have a better opportunity to make a decent living, which requires better access to DC markets, a better return on commodity exports, a massive shift of manufacturing capacity from DCs to LDCs, a greater share of world trade in manufactures, improved access to capital markets, and increased capital transfers, especially medium- and long-term transfers. Not only would the NIEO generate development in the LDCs and raise their living standards, it would pull glutted, stagnating northern economies out of their slump by providing new markets, promote a better international division of labor, and, by maximizing economic efficiency, help to reduce worldwide inflation.

One should not overlook the noneconomic aspects of the NIEO, for they tell us, perhaps better than anything else, what the North-South dialogue is all about. Running through every document, the NIEO Declaration, and the CERDS is a call for justice, for fairness, for equity, for independence. Third World nations have emerged only recently from generations of domination and, because of that domination, a deep sense of humiliation. What those nations cherish above all is status and respect. They thought they had gained it with political independence, only to find that political independence rests upon a foundation of economic viability. So they still feel exploited and, rightly or wrongly, blame their poverty on a world economic system that they believe denies them a fair return for their resources and labor while draining most of the profits off into the hands of the capitalists—a situation that provides a field day for Marxist economics. But beyond the theory and the economics is that far-off universal goal of a fair break and the achievement of status and respect.

The NIEO is also, and more familiarly, a process that involves means and methods. The means for effecting the proposed radical changes are, understandably, multitudinous and detailed, and they affect every sector of economic life. Briefly, they include:

Trade: better access to DC markets, including an expanded and liberalized generalized system of preferences (GSP), reduction of tariffs and nontariff barriers (NTBS), elimination of restrictive business practices (RBPS), higher commodity prices, more processing in LDCs, financial schemes to compensate for export fluctuations, establishment of a Common Fund, and new international commodity agreements

Finance: reform of the international monetary system, automatic and assured aid, reduced conditionality, the special drawing right (SDR)/aid link, a world tax on seabed resources, increased and liberalized official development assistance (ODA), expansion of development banks, improved export financing, and balance-of-payments support

Development: more processing in LDCs, transfers of manufacture to LDCs, transfer of technology, and regulation of transnational corporations

These examples are only suggestive of all the means proposed. All of the measures are interrelated, and any single one could be considered as supportive of development, finance, or trade. Obviously, they have to be seen in an integrated way. Nor does the NIEO stop with such central matters. It also includes plans for oceans, space, communications, economic cooperation among developing countries, food, and shipping—all are important but only as facets of the central idea.

Supporting the means are special methods since, as President Nyerere observed, a new economic system "will not happen through the workings of laissez-faire."[4] By looking at some of the methods proposed, we can get a better idea of what most of the argument is about. The methods vary: producer cartels, such as OPEC, to set prices by supply management and to force consumer nations (DCs) to make desired changes; international negotiations, e.g., the CIEC and UN forums; Third World unity to maintain majority pressures in the United Nations and other negotiating forums; new funds to effect transfers; changes in international law; horse trading within the system, e.g., linkage of one issue to another; public opinion; increased membership in international bodies, e.g., the IMF, World Bank, and the International Atomic Energy Agency (IAEA); more international organizations; more international management. None of these methods have been particularly "successful" so far. At this stage, the "chosen instrument" seems to be the UN system backed up by OPEC, with UNCTAD as the key agency for negotiating (if it can be called that) concessions from the developed countries.

There is argument and confrontation on all levels—from top to bottom, from theory to practice, from ends to means to methods. Indeed, the various elements, here neatly disaggregated, are usually so scrambled together that it is impossible to separate ends from means, especially when the protagonists are locked in argument about totally different things—in a dialogue of the deaf. But on the lower level, the methods proposed to change the world, one can perceive most of the action at the negotiating table. The UNCTAD V negotiations can show how the various elements interact and what is and is not ultimately decisive.

Interdependence

Item 8 of the UNCTAD V agenda, "Interdependence," addressed the theme of the conference, "Restructuring the International Economic System," and because that item attempted an evaluation of progress toward the NIEO, it provided a dress rehearsal for the 1980 special session of the General Assembly. Interdependence was included on the agenda over the objections of Group B, which had wanted it merged into the general debate, and the wording of Item 8 had been one of the most contentious points negotiated at the Trade and Development Board (TDB) meeting in September 1978.[5]

Documentation for the item included two special studies, the first being a restatement of the need for a new international economic order.[6] The existing international system had failed to provide adequate support for LDC development efforts, and little progress had been made toward the establishment of the NIEO. The world was now going through an economic crisis, and the LDCs were having to bear a disproportionate share of the burden of adjustment. The DCs assumed that the key to the solution lay in their own economic recovery—a return to the processes at work in the economy before 1974—but that assumption failed to recognize the existence of any links between the economic difficulties of the DCs and the underlying structural disequilibrium in the existing international division of labor and the trading and financial system. If the DCs did recognize that link, they would see that the primary means to achieve stable and sustained economic recovery would be through restructuring. Necessary changes, therefore, included new international consultation mechanisms to help harmonize national policies; reform of the trading rules; global economic management to allow the international community to exercise a significant influence on the pattern and direction of world trade flows; and negotiation of a new international economic convention, an updated version of the Havana charter,[7] that would embody all the separate aspects of the NIEO.

The second study[8] concentrated on the need to consider development in the wider context of the interrelated issues of global economic relations. The first and second development decades had taken this view, and measures to aid the LDCs had been seen as exemptions from the "rules of the game" granted for the purpose of speeding up the process of their "graduation" to full partnership in the global system. That idea had not worked because the DCs had failed to fulfill the role envisaged for them. What was required, therefore, was a broad overview of the management of the world economy. A high-level advisory group should be established that would make recommendations to the Trade and Development Board to bring actual policies into harmony with the requirements of structural change. Such a group would enable the TDB to make *political* decisions that would lead to an improvement in the functioning of the world economy.

The Arusha Programme[9] repeated the ideas, recommendations, and even the language of the UNCTAD documentation. Although it antedated the UNCTAD V documents by more than a month (February 28), it was, obviously, mainly the work of the UNCTAD Secretariat so there was little difference between them. However, the Arusha Programme also included the explicit complaint that LDCs have little to say in the decision-making process of the international economic order, and it attacked the concept of basic needs.

According to the U.S. delegation's instructions,[10] the developed countries of the OECD were sympathetic to the LDCs' complaint about the current economic situation but did not agree with the analysis. They agreed that the world economic system was not perfect and accepted the need for an evolving international economic system with the twin goals of efficiency and equity to meet the needs of all countries, including the LDCs. However, the system had changed considerably in the previous three decades, often in response to the growing importance of the developing countries. Moreover, structural adjustment was occurring, with the market system acting generally as an efficient arbitrator. The proposals of the G-77 for negotiations on structural adjustment would be counterproductive.

Although the G-77 members believed that international factors were the prime determinants of development, the DCs believed that individual governments were primarily responsible for the success or failure of their own development. International aid could help, but the critical factors were individual management and economic policies. The object of development was not resources transfer, therefore, but an improvement in the lives of the people. The United States hoped that the North-South dialogue would address the real issues of development rather than engage in sterile rhetoric and discussions of nonnegotiable demands. The work of UNCTAD should be more relevant to the immediate concerns of poor people and poor countries and less concerned with the international system.

The United States did not favor the idea of a high-level advisory group. First, such a group would appear to duplicate the UNGA Committee of the Whole (COW), which had been created in 1977 as a follow-up forum to the CIEC. Second, many North-South issues were already the responsibility of the IMF, IBRD, and GATT, not of UNCTAD.

Negotiations bogged down on the first day of the conference, "in time-consuming but unilluminating sessions," over the preambular texts of competing G-77, Australian, and Group B resolutions. The delegates focused finally on a G-77 recommendation for global consultations and an "experts group," but that recommendation ran into Group B opposition, and the G-77 was unable to explain how a new consulting group would be an improvement over the present system. The Soviets were against the recommendation, the Latin Americans wanted to oppose it to make the point that global negotiations could not take place unless energy was on the agenda, and the G-77 representatives from the United Nations were disinclined to enhance Corea's reputation.[11]

In the end, the drafting group for Item 8 remanded the entire item to the next meeting of the TDB. The United States was not displeased, because it had avoided undue recriminations from the G-77 who were badly split; avoided any commitment to a new institution; and gotten the energy issue, which had been kept off the agenda, flagged for attention.[12] The remanding of Item 8 was a disappointment for the G-77 and the UNCTAD Secretariat, because that item would have provided the conceptual framework to underlie all other policy issues covered by the agenda and interdependence was the theme of UNCTAD V.[13] In its report to Washington, the U.S. delegation blamed the failure to achieve agreement on Item 8 generally on a disagreement among the LDCs over how to deal with energy, "the hidden item on the agenda," and particularly on the opposition of the OPEC countries.[14]

Trade

UNCTAD V had a wide range of subjects to consider under trade, including trade in manufactures, protectionism and adjustment, the MTNs, commodities, the GSP, and RBPs. All the subjects interlocked, which presented problems of coordination, sorting out, and duplication. Discussions were slow in starting as the G-77 took two weeks for the internal processing of its draft resolutions.[15] The commodities negotiating group processed a number of minor resolutions first, while working steadily on an omnibus resolution covering the Common Fund, the IPC, compensatory finance, marketing and distribution, and processing. Since those most difficult topics came last, they were negotiated under considerable time pressure.[16]

The G-77 blamed the DCs for increasing protectionism, which, it said, was costing the LDCs billions of dollars in trade lost and slowing down development. The G-77 demanded better access to DC markets, positive adjustment, adoption of a set of principles to safeguard LDC interests in the short term, a "long-term framework agreement" on principles to govern structural adjustment, and an UNCTAD surveillance system to monitor progress.[17] The Arusha Programme recommended that the rules and principles be negotiated through UNCTAD and linked to the Lima targets for achieving 25 percent of world manufacturing and 30 percent of world trade in manufactures for LDCs by the year 2000.[18]

The United States and the OECD countries officially opposed protectionism and favored positive adjustment, but the United States stressed that adjustment was the responsibility of all countries. It supported a resolution, therefore, but with the proviso that "no country can give up the right to protect its workers and industries through temporary measures."[19] In the final compromise resolution, the LDCs agreed to drop the more mandatory and *dirigiste* aspects they had demanded, including giving UNCTAD a central role in monitoring adjustment and organizing negotiations.[20]

The United States had also hoped to get a resolution endorsing the Tokyo Round negotiations, which it called the most ambitious and the most successful round of negotiations in the history of the GATT and which, it declared, would lay the foundation for the world trading system for the next twenty years.[21] But the LDCs rejected the U.S. assertion completely, claiming that the MTNs had failed to live up to the objectives of the Tokyo Declaration of September 1973. They had refused to sign the final trade agreement in April 1979, pointing out that it had no legal authority to enforce the new rules and that the LDCs had not been sufficiently included in the negotiations. They were dissatisfied with the action on selective safeguards, tropical products, agriculture, NTBS, the erosion of the GSP, and the overall international framework.[22] The LDCs called for a reopening of the negotiations and for the adoption of the MTNs and codes by consensus of all countries,[23] demands that were totally unacceptable to the DCs, which had sweated to get any agreement at all and were not about to open up the negotiations again.

The failure to get Third World endorsement of the MTNs, etc., represented a standoff between DCs and LDCs on the world trading system. The LDCs rejected a GATT-type negotiation, and the DCs rejected demands for a new trading order. The UNCTAD document "The Multilateral Trade Negotiations" recommended that UNCTAD carry out an evaluation of the

MTNs in terms of the NIEO and CERDS and that the conference adopt a set of principles to govern trade relations between DCs and LDCs (paragraph 142). The Arusha Programme recommended a new legal framework for trade and a shifting of the focus of trade away from GATT and over to UNCTAD. Adding these measures to those recommended under protectionism and adjustment would have brought all trade matters under UNCTAD auspices, subjected them to NIEO standards, and set the pace and nature of structural adjustment. In a nutshell, the Arusha Programme demanded DC acceptance of UN control and supervision of trade and adjustment, a situation no DC, let alone the United States, would or could accept.

If growth of manufactures and trade in manufactures are the aspirations of the Third World, trade in commodities is its livelihood accounting for over 80 percent of LDC exports (including fuels) and up to 95 percent of LLDC exports.[24] The object of the G-77 at Manila was to push for a commitment to complete the Common Fund articles negotiations; rapidly complete negotiations on other commodities under the IPC, including "across-the-board negotiations"; create a complementary finance facility; expand processing in the LDCs under a "comprehensive framework"; and improve LDC marketing and distribution systems under a "framework for international cooperation,"[25] consisting mainly of DC commitments, assurances and agreements, and guidelines for more funding and technical assistance.[26]

The U.S. position was that it was technically too early to start negotiations on all commodities and that negotiations should be between producers and consumers. The LDC contention that the DCs were dragging their feet was rejected. On LDC processing, the United States believed that comparative advantage and market economics should be the basic determinants rather than international management. It warned of the "formidably intellectual problems" of the whole commodities picture; rejected a broadened UNCTAD mandate in the commodity field, e.g., "comprehensive frameworks"; and flatly opposed the creation of a compensatory finance facility as "inappropriate"—since there were already three (IMF, the European Community LDC export commodity stabilization system [STABEX], and the Arab Monetary Fund)—until the results were known of an IMF/IBRD study of the whole question.[27]

The result was a watered down omnibus resolution (124[V]) with U.S. and Group B reservations to any "commitments" beyond what had already been agreed during the Common Fund negotiations and at UNCTAD IV. But the G-77, in a surprise move that angered Group B countries, deleted the section on a compensatory finance facility and passed it as a separate resolution over DC objections (125[V]).

Without judging the merits of either side's point of view, it can be said that the commodity negotiations were fundamentally negotiations between protection of the free-market system and its institutions on the one hand and a more managed and perhaps more equitable, but not necessarily more "economic," international system on the other. Furthermore, it is quite evident that economic growth was not the sole object, that the diplomatic world was still sorting out the political control and distribution of increasingly scarce resources. Commodity problems came to the negotiating table heavily burdened with political considerations.

Item 11 of the agenda, "Manufactures and Semimanufactures," served to cover the GSP, RBPs, and a "comprehensive strategy" to promote LDC trade in manufactures. This item added to the confusion because it overlapped with previous items, but it provided the opportunity to launch another UNCTAD scheme for economic management. The basic problem, according to UNCTAD documentation, was an "unbridgeable dilemma" for LDCs. On the one hand, they could not compete with the TNCs in capital-intensive production and trade, and on the other hand, they were kept out of the markets for labor-intensive goods by DC protectionism, labor unions, and sluggish demand.[28] The only solution was a comprehensive strategy that included adoption of the Lima targets, a reexamination and reform of DC trade policies, positive adjustment, a phasing out of declining industries, improvement of LDC manufacturing and processing, and control of TNCs, plus a DC-LDC "framework agreement" to assure compliance, funding, and technical assistance by DCs.[29]

The result was a failed resolution that was referred to the TDB for further consideration. Group B countries rejected the G-77 proposals on the grounds that opportunities for growth were being provided through the MTNs and the GSP, that positive adjustment was taking place in the DCs, and that it was now up to the LDCs to take advantage of the opportunities. Many countries—e.g., Taiwan, Singapore, Brazil, and Korea—had already made remarkable gains by doing just that.[30]

The treatment of restrictive business practices (RBPs) was perfunctory. The subject had been under scrutiny in UNCTAD for years, and negotiations had been under way on a set of rules and principles for a model law on RBPs. The job of UNCTAD V was to set the date for a conference that would negotiate and prepare for the adoption of rules and principles for RBP controls.[31]

There was little problem with this topic, and the resolution on RBPs (103[V]) was one of two resolutions to survive in Negotiating Group 2 (Trade). The United States and Group B already had an OECD set of rules and principles and had gingerly favored an UNCTAD-negotiated agreement with the LDCs, providing the agreement worked both ways. The facts that the resolution only provided for holding a conference and did not go into the substantive differences over the legal nature of the rules and that the G-77 dropped its demands for an extensive new range of studies by UNCTAD and the creation of a new UNCTAD committee on RBPs helped.[32] (The United States and Group B countries were absolutely opposed to mandatory rules or to any new machinery.)

The GSP agreements are due for renegotiation by the EC countries in 1981 (by the United States and Canada in 1985), so UNCTAD V provided a timely occasion for the G-77 to lay its demands on the table. The G-77 called for assurances that the GSP would be extended and product coverage liberalized, and also requested bilateral negotiation of product withdrawals and safeguards, nondiscrimination among LDCs, and compensation for the erosion of preference margins by the MTNS.[33]

The initiative failed. The United States and other Group B countries considered the GSP nonnegotiable, a temporary and unilateral concession, and rejected the idea of compensation for erosion of preference margins or for channeling GSP negotiations into UNCTAD. The DC philosophy was that no country should have permanent differential status and that the GSP was a temporary advantage given unilaterally to disadvantaged countries to help them climb up to a competitive level.[34] Furthermore, although it might appear that the Group B countries were being overly legalistic in their position, the Group B attitude has to be assessed in the light of its alternative, which would involve channeling GSP negotiations into UNCTAD and placing the rules and principles of operation under multilateral control.

In summary, little was achieved on trade items at UNCTAD V. The Group B countries would not reopen the MTNS or turn the GSP schemes over to UNCTAD. The extreme demands for a DC structural adjustment were reduced to having UNCTAD do an annual review of the subject. There was agreement on protectionism and on holding a conference to negotiate a code on RBPs.

Concerning manufacturing, several G-77 initiatives to mount special UNCTAD programs to promote LDC manufacturing, processing, and marketing capacity foundered on the reef of DC objections to expanding UNCTAD budgets or authority. With respect to commodities, a package of measures, including a framework for cooperation to promote marketing and distribution and comprehensive measures to support manufacturing, failed and was sent back to the TDB. The one substantial result, obtained over dogged DC resistance, was the provision for an UNCTAD study of a complementary finance facility for commodity trade stabilization.

Divested of their international machinery, the demands of the LDCs seem to be reasonable: more manufacturing and processing capacity; marketing, finance, and distribution facilities; fair access to world markets; and fair treatment in the trading community. But the LDCs blame their problems on "the system," so future progress depends on a NIEO. At this stage, the "reasonable objectives" of the LDCs begin to seem "unreasonable" to the DCs. Opening up the international order has been difficult, but it cannot be denied that many concessions and facilities have been provided. Reforming the international order, changing the ground rules to take more account of the LDCs, is going to be extremely difficult. Replacing the present order by a NIEO would appear to be impossible, especially by the means suggested, that is, through UNCTAD.

Monetary and Financial Issues

The financial aspects of development and North-South relations are at once the most well known and the least understood. They are well known because they directly involve financial transfers from the DCs where the aid budgets are subject to annual debate in national legislatures. They are least understood because general knowledge seldom penetrates below the surface into the relatively arcane realms of international banking, monetary operations, and public finance with which the otherwise straightforward business of aid has become entangled. And that is where the problem lies. As the LDCs develop and are knitted into the international system, they are more and more profoundly affected by international forces that are beyond their control—by world monetary instability, inflation, accumulating debt, payments imbalances, and export shortfalls—which are becoming more controversial than even the amounts and quality of resource transfers.

Item 12A, "International Monetary Reform," was a catchall item that was partly philosophical and partly operational. LDC balance-of-payments problems were blamed on structural (not cyclic) imbalances in the international economy, and the international monetary system had to be adapted accordingly. That would mean better medium- and long-term balance-of-payments financing through a new multilateral facility and a liberalization of IMF conditionality geared to short-term imbalances.[35] The Arusha Programme endorsed the UNCTAD recommendations and called for a new Marshall Plan for the Third World, the establishment of an intergovernmental high-level group of experts within UNCTAD to study the "evolution" of the international monetary system, and the holding of a conference on international monetary reform.[36]

The United States takes an old-fashioned, no-nonsense position on monetary affairs. It sees G-77 demands as an attempt to turn the IMF into another development agency, to weaken its autonomy, and to transfer power to UNCTAD. The United States insists that the IMF maintain its role as the world's central monetary institution and that monetary issues be discussed and negotiated only within the IMF framework. Although favoring a liberalization of the IMF Compensatory Finance Facility, the United States believes that strict conditionality is essential and rejects the demand for a new balance-of-payments facility. "Changes in the IMF not consistent with its basic purpose will adversely affect its ability to foster *the open and healthy world economy* essential to LDC development" (italics mine).[37] Finally, the United States rejects the idea of a high-level group of experts or any implication that negotiations can take place outside the IMF.

The G-77, however, meant business and, over Group B opposition, passed Resolution 128(V), "International Monetary Reform," which repeated the recommendations of the Arusha Programme. The U.S. delegation regretted the outcome and believed that a compromise closer to the U.S. position could have been achieved. It felt its failure was because its own instructions had been too rigid and because it had to reserve its position on questions currently under study by the IMF.[38]

The subject of resource transfers is a hardy perennial; the LDCs lay on the pressure, and the DCs do their best to limit the damage, real or cosmetic. UNCTAD V called for all Development Assistance Committee (DAC) members to increase ODA to the 0.7 percent of GNP target of the Second Development Decade and to improve ODA terms, for multilateral development banks (MDBS) to tailor policies and practices to "internationally agreed objectives for development," and for private capital to extend more favorable terms to LDCs.[39] The Arusha Programme also demanded that donors make binding commitments to raise ODA levels; that ODA be put on an increasingly assured, continuous, and automatic basis; that MDBS be expanded and their programs liberalized; that private capital give LDCs preferential treatment and allow for increased local participation and the creation of a multilateral loan guarantee facility.[40]

The United States has never accepted the 0.7 percent ODA target, and the U.S. delegation could not negotiate on the terms or conditions of ODA, which is within the purview of the Congress. The United States favored increases in the resources of MDBS but not interference in their structure and policies. With regard to private capital, U.S. government influence is limited since markets are private by definition. The major burden, therefore, rests with the LDC governments to create a favorable investment climate. The United States rejected the proposal for new institutions, e.g., a multilateral guarantee facility, and the idea of massive transfers was out of the question.[41]

Despite differences, UNCTAD V passed a watered down consensus resolution (129[V]), which reaffirmed the 0.7 percent target, set standards for ODA quality, made recommendations for improvement in the management of MDBS and for means to facilitate LDC access to private capital markets, including measures to generate "massive transfers."[42] For the United States, the resolution was a moderate loss. The U.S. delegation succeeded in muting strong criticism of the United States but failed to hold the line at what had been agreed on in the United Nations as a common DC/LDC position. As a consequence, the United States had to make reservations in the final plenary session, restating its basic position. The U.S. delegation also felt constrained to explain the failure to Washington on the grounds that during the last thirty-six hours of the conference the Africans had walked out, which stalled the process of negotiation and made amendments to the provisional text virtually impossible.[43]

Those deliberations on resource transfers are as good an example as any of a "nonnegotiation." The sources of funds are the U.S. Congress on bilateral matters, other countries, the MDBS, and private capital markets — over none of which does the Department of State have any direct authority. What the department can and did do was to resist any implication of international direction of policy or any recommendation for new international funds or organizations. The State Department tried but failed to reaffirm the importance of the investment climate for private sector flows.

The long-standing proposal for an export credit guarantee facility (ECGF) briefly surfaced but was again submerged by common consent for bureaucratic reasons. However, that proposal illustrates the classic U.S. problem with G-77/UNCTAD proposals in the financial area. The idea of an ECGF was to make it easier for LDC exporters to discount commercial paper at favorable terms and without the long waiting period for direct payment.[44] However, the United States continues to oppose an ECGF, because it believes that many questions still remain to be answered on the details of structure, how such a facility would function, which countries would benefit, and which types of exports would be covered. The United States questions whether an ECGF would be a high-priority use of scarce resources, especially since the poorest LDCs would be in no position to use it. The United States also believes that it would be a mistake to tamper with international capital markets when there are more direct ways to deal with such payments.[45]

Third World debt is becoming one of the most emotive facets of the North-South dialogue; it is fraught with dire predictions and is an increasingly political issue between DCs, OPEC, and LDCs. Opinions differ on the seriousness of the world debt situation. Some groups believe that the increasing costs of oil and manufactured goods will push many LDCs to the point of default; others (including the United States, the World Bank, and the IMF) believe that — certain countries excepted — LDC debt is not unmanageable when inflation and export growth are taken into account. However, a danger point may be reached in the early eighties when the short-term loans to non-oil-exporting LDCs to cover the higher costs of oil imports come due. The issue is whether to demand strict adherence to debt terms and IMF conditionality or whether such a demand would only further depress the LDCs' evolution toward economic viability.

UNCTAD's TDB Resolution 165 (S-IX) recommended retroactive terms adjustment (RTA) of past loans to the poorer LDCs and identified debt features concepts that recognize that debt reorganization should be "development oriented." The UNCTAD V documentation went a step further, calling for an independent debt commission for research into and management of debt problems and recommending that DC creditor clubs be transformed into a truly international mechanism.[46] The Arusha Programme endorsed the UNCTAD proposals, but it rejected any effort to bifurcate debt problems into acute and long-term (that is, into balance-of-payments and structural) problems and stressed that domestic correction measures "do not give external authorities the right to infringe on the sovereignty of states [conditionality]."[47]

The basic U.S. position was that there was no generalized LDC debt problem. There had, indeed, been a considerable increase in the external debt of the non-oil-exporting LDCs, but that did not produce a major debt servicing problem (debt payment as a percentage of export income). Acute problems were then restricted to only a few countries — viz., Afghanistan (30 percent), Brazil (40 percent), Mexico (24 percent), Argentina (28 percent), and Peru (27 percent)[48] — and, for the near future, the situation would remain the same. The wide diversity of debtor country situations fully justified the traditional case-by-case approach rather than the across-the-board approach recommended by the LDCs.[49] The United States was philosophically opposed to the idea of debt cancellation, because that would violate the international system and set an unmanageable precedent. The United States would, however, consider RTA to those countries on the UN list of thirty relatively least developed countries, but on a case-by-case basis. Proposed U.S. legislation would make it possible for recipient countries to funnel debt repayments into local currency accounts for development.[50] Nor did the United States favor a debt commission; the present system was working well, and outside of some low-income LDCs that believed that such a commission might generate increased resource transfers, there was no great support for one among the LDCs themselves, especially among the higher-income LDCs such as Mexico and Brazil that believed that debt relief would harm their credit worthiness on international capital markets.[51]

Prolonged negotiation among what became known as the "debt set" failed to result in any agreement. The G-77 resolution ran into solid Group B opposition and was eventually sent on to the permanent machinery of

UNCTAD. Group B remained solidly against a wider UNCTAD role, major restructuring of credit group procedures, or new institutional mechanisms. A Group B counterresolution was withdrawn.[52] Creditor group integrity was preserved, and no commitment was made for future UNCTAD work on debt.[53]

The last item under monetary issues was "International Financial Cooperation," a proposal for an international fund for trade and development (IFTD). The proposed fund would complement the present monetary system rather than change it by providing a new institution to coordinate and rationalize financial transfers to LDCs. The present system, it was asserted, had failed to meet LDC financial requirements, especially for soft and long-term balance-of-payments support and compensatory finance. Furthermore, the present system was creditor oriented, not truly international. An IFTD would provide a global overview of LDC needs, international or "democratic" management, grants to the least developed countries, financing for shortfalls in export earnings, investment financing for export related investment, and a multilateral export credit guarantee facility.[54] The Arusha Programme repeated those recommendations and emphasized that an IFTD would provide a multilateral framework for debt operations, give LDCs an equitable share in the decision making, and assure adequate long-term flows for balance-of-payments support and compensatory finance. It recommended that UNCTAD V approve those basic elements with further work by a group of experts.[55]

A G-77 resolution, not surprisingly, met with solid Group B opposition and was referred back to the TDB.[56] The United States maintained that the existing structure of international financial cooperation was sufficiently diversified to respond to any situation, including LDC development; that there was coordination in the system; that no international organization could "guarantee" the achievement of LDC development objectives; that the competence of the existing international institutions should not be impaired; and that it was important to respect free initiative and to preserve the flexibility of private capital.[57] The existing system could be improved by better coordination and by increased levels of concessional lending, but basically, it provided the best mechanism to respond to economic needs and realities.[58]

The item on international financial cooperation brought together several subjects treated separately under other agenda items, particularly items 8 ("Interdependence"), 12A ("International Monetary Reform"), 12B ("Resource Transfers"), and 12D ("Debt"). What was new was the composite picture presented. A new fund, a group of experts, a multilateral framework (in UNCTAD), and a system of financing similar to national social security were drawn together into a "democratically" managed, complementary system largely funded by DC sources — a monetary equivalent of the comprehensive world trade system already discussed.

In summary, Item 12, "Monetary and Financial Issues," purported to cover the broad range of international monetary reform and cooperation. The focus of the item, however, was maintaining LDC financial liquidity and development growth in spite of inflation, debt, oil price increases, conditionality and ODA decline. The LDCs pointed out that since their development difficulties were due to international problems beyond their powers to change, the system should insulate the LDCs and provide the means to ensure their continued development according to UN development and strategy targets. Although the plan should include various measures to ameliorate the constraints in the present system, the long-range objective must be to provide for an alternative system that is geared more closely to LDC requirements. But, compared to the grand design outlined in "International Financial Cooperation," the achievements at UNCTAD V were minimal.

Basically, what divides DCs and LDCs is strength and confidence. The DCs take the turbulence of free international economic life for granted and more or less in stride. Built into the capitalist system is the assumption of risk; profits are, or used to be, considered the reward for risk taking. But behind many LDC recommendations is the demand for riskless development; for security; for an assured, dependable, and automatic flow of resources; for insulation from the turbulent and unforgiving open world; for guarantees against loss, setback, failure, or accident. It is an oft-repeated DC complaint that "They want to have the benefits, but want us to take all the risks." Under the circumstances, it is no wonder that U.S. appeals to preserve the great free-market system fall on deaf or indifferent ears. That, it would seem, is exactly what the LDCs do not want.

Transfer of Technology

Although technology for development — from swords to plowshares — has been a subject of interest and controversy for decades, it received new impetus during the seventies as the LDCs became more acutely aware that one of the main obstacles to their growth was their low level of technological skill and the difficulty of acquiring such skill. Thus, among the basic principles of the NIEO is the aim of "giving developing countries access to the achievements of modern science and technology and the creation of indigenous technology."[59] That objective has been woven into many strands of the North-South negotiations, and it was the major topic of the UN Conference on Science and Technology for Development (UNCSTD), which was convened in August 1979 in Vienna (see Chapter 5). UNCTAD V took up four aspects of the subject: a code of conduct on the transfer of technology, industrial property (patents and trademarks), the brain drain, and, inevitably, an UNCTAD proposal for a global transfer-of-technology system and a new fund.

There had already been over three years of negotiations on a code of conduct, which had been called for in April 1976 by UNCTAD IV Resolution 89(IV) aimed principally at multinational corporations. Several issues divided DCS and LDCS, but none more so than the legal nature of the code, with the DCS aiming for a voluntary code and the LDCS insisting on a mandatory one. A four-week UN conference in October 1978 had resumed during February and March 1979, but it failed to reach any agreement.[60]

The G-77 nations were frustrated and unhappy. They said that the code of conduct, along with the IPC and the Common Fund, is one of the key instruments for achieving the objectives of the NIEO, and they blamed the DCS for a lack of political will.[61] But Group B had tried. At first Group B had opposed both international supervisory machinery and a mandatory code. During the March 1979 meeting, they had conceded on the supervisory mechanism, expecting the G-77, in return, to concede on the legal application.[62] But the G-77, which continued to feel that it had made all the concessions and had shown the only "political will," refused to compromise.[63]

No further progress on a code of conduct was made at UNCTAD V, and no resolution was adopted. Group B tried to effect a new compromise by recommending voluntary guidelines and, if they did not work, a review of all aspects of the code at a later date. The G-77 refused the recommendation, proposing instead another conference in five years' time, with a "view to transforming the code into a legally binding instrument." Group B rejected that proposal, so there was nothing to do but defer the issue until a second session of the UN conference was held in the autumn.[64]

Later, a diplomatic conference convened in Geneva in 1980 under the auspices of the World Intellectual Property Organization (WIPO) to revise the eighty-eight-member Paris Convention for the Protection of Industrial Property, the most important multinational treaty concerning industrial property, which specifies certain minimum levels of protection to be provided for patents and trademarks by member countries. The developing world, however, saw the convention as the basis for legally abusing the rights and interests of developing countries through the control of trademarks and patents. But the problem was widely recognized, and the revision of the Paris Convention was, for the first time, to include special provisions to protect the interest of the LDCS.

The issue at UNCTAD V was principally the extent to which UNCTAD should play a role in the industrial property field. UNCTAD has had a mandate since UNCTAD III (Santiago 1972) to ensure that any revision of the industrial property system took LDC interests into account,[65] but the United States and Group B regarded WIPO as the only intergovernmental organization to have the responsibility of maintaining and revising the Paris Convention. UNC-TAD's role, therefore, should be strictly limited to that of a consultant on matters having a bearing on the development aspects of the industrial property system.[66]

Negotiations at UNCTAD V focused on a G-77 attempt to negotiate important substantive issues reserved for negotiation at the diplomatic conference,[67] and a resolution was adopted. Resolution 101(V) reiterated the basic principles and interests of UNCTAD and the G-77 in the revision of the patent system, emphasized special considerations of interest to the LDCs with regard to trademarks, urged all states that were members of UNCTAD to attend the Geneva conference, and invited the UNCTAD secretary-general to continue UNCTAD's work on the economic, commercial, and development aspects of industrial property.[68]

The main substantive business concerning technology was the secretariat's ambitious proposals for a new technology fund, a world system to effect technological transfers to LDCs, and an enhancement of UNCTAD's resources to carry out its responsibilities. The system would include technology centers and staffs on national, regional, interregional, and international levels to effect and coordinate planning for institutional development, training, R&D, and sectoral needs, with the ultimate objective of reducing LDC dependence by increasing LDC technological capacity.[69] The Arusha Programme added the requirement that the DCs report on their implementation of the transfer of technology and that UNCTAD V should decide on "concrete modalities" to keep DC compliance under continuing review.[70]

The United States, with a long-standing commitment to LDC technological development, had supported the creation of national centers and the establishment of an UNCTAD advisory service to provide technical assistance to the LDCs. However, the United States did not agree with UNCTAD's increasing emphasis on the "threats and benefits" of the external system while overlooking the importance and opportunities of developing indigenous technology, particularly toward meeting basic needs. Nor did the United States agree that UNCTAD needs more money, thinking that UNCTAD would do better to make effective use of the money it already has and avoid duplicating or preempting the work of other UN bodies.[71]

Nevertheless, the conference passed Resolution 112(V), which provided for the essential idea proposed by the secretariat but without a new technology fund or an enlargement of the UNCTAD advisory service.[72] The secretary-general "will invite" DC governments to report on the implementation of their responsibilities. The reservations are revealing. The G-77 specified that a reference to technology for the lower strata of the world's population did not imply an endorsement of the concept of "basic needs."[73] Group B stated that it did not endorse the eventual creation of a technology fund or the idea of a "comprehensive global strategy," and it reserved its position on all matters involving the financial implications of the proposed UNCTAD program.[74]

Developing countries have watched helplessly as badly needed professionals, doctors, engineers, and scientists have "defected" to the West. UNCTAD estimated that during the sixties and seventies over 420,000 professionals emigrated, mainly to the United States, Canada, and the United Kingdom but also to Europe, Australia, and New Zealand and mostly from the Philippines, Pakistan, Syria, Iran, India, and Sri Lanka. It was estimated, for example, that from 50 percent to 70 percent of the annual output of Pakistani doctors, about 25 percent of the annual output of Indian engineers, and about 30 percent of Indian doctors emigrated annually.[75]

In 1977 the Thirty-second General Assembly had passed a resolution that called on UNCTAD to conduct a feasibility study for the establishment of an international mechanism by which DCs would compensate LDCs for their loss of skilled manpower, and UNCTAD went ahead with studies for a "global brain-drain tax." The Arusha Programme made a relatively innocuous statement that called for a "comprehensive approach" and action by UNCTAD.[76]

The United States supported studies of the brain-drain problem but was opposed to any compensation scheme. Its position was that the problem was a complex one, it could not be remedied by any system of international financial compensation, and it could best be ameliorated through national or bilateral action. Further, the United States believed that ECOSOC and the UN Secretariat in New York, with possible help from the International Labour Organisation (ILO), the World Health Organization (WHO), and the United Nations Educational, Scientific, and Cultural Organization (UNESCO), were best suited to study the problem, and the State Department was concerned that such work would divert "valuable resources from UNCTAD's fundamental task of economic development."[77]

Negotiations were mainly between Group B and the UNCTAD Secretariat, the prime mover of the scheme, and few G-77 countries were even interested, except for Jordan, which had introduced the scheme in 1977. The secretariat wanted a firm mandate; Group B was solidly opposed.[78] A consensus resolution (102[V]) was finally adopted, which provided for further work by the United Nations and UNCTAD but brought in the compensation scheme only obliquely and did not imply endorsement by Group B.

Summary and Comment

A purposeful, long-term, worldwide cooperative endeavor to force the pace of technological transfer must certainly be one of the most intelligent, enlightened ideas of the century. The implications are enormous. Technology is capital in a concentrated form, so that a small injection of technology may have the effect of masses of capital investment. Indeed, a sustained program of technology transfer may achieve the result envisaged by a massive transfer of capital in a fraction of the time. Such a program may even make the difference between life or death, as technology for food and energy may save some countries and peoples from ultimate disaster.

Unfortunately, the results of UNCTAD V do not give the impression that great strides forward were made. A code of conduct was left on the negotiating table, and the resolutions on the brain drain and industrial property were innocuous at best. Resolution 112(V) on the transfer of technology could, indeed, have far-reaching implications, depending on whether the declared purposes are effectively served. Perhaps most disappointing was the trivializing of a great purpose. The turgid and all but incomprehensible language of the UNCTAD resolutions, the haggling for small advantage, and the ubiquitous bureaucratic ambitions of UNCTAD seemed to suck the very life out of the endeavor rather than nourishing and enhancing it. In all fairness, the mediocrity of the UNCTAD V achievement on technology could have been at least partly the fault of the forthcoming UN Conference on Science and Technology for Development (UNCSTD). Countries would not go to the mat in Manila if they thought they might do better in Vienna.

Economic Cooperation Among Developing Countries (ECDC)

If UNCTAD V had a theme beyond the global management visions of UNCTAD itself, it was surely LDC unity and self-reliance. President of Tanzania Nyerere, in his opening speech at Arusha, had emphasized time and again the priority of unity, whatever else happened.[79] The Arusha Programme was entitled "Programme for Collective Self-Reliance," first, and, second, a "Framework for Negotiations." The ministers declared in paragraph 1 that they had met "to reaffirm our spirit of solidarity and collective self-reliance,"[80] and they stressed that collective self-reliance was an integral part of the global economic system and "an essential element of . . . the restructuring of international economic relations."[81]

Agenda Item 18, "Economic Cooperation Among Developing Countries" (ECDC), therefore carried considerable weight and had more than mere economic implications. ECDC was one of the basic aspects of the NIEO,[82] and, although several earlier cooperative schemes — e.g., the East African and the Central American common markets — had failed, the NIEO gave the idea new life. The NIEO Declaration in 1974 was followed by the Manila Declaration in 1976, which led to Resolution 92(IV) at Nairobi in May 1976 and the adoption of a Program of Action by a G-77 conference on ECDC in Mexico City in September 1976. That Progam of Action provided the conceptual basis for subsequent work covering preferential trade arrangements, coordinated production and marketing enterprises, regional resource development, LDC banking and financial schemes, and a variety of joint economic enterprises.[83]

UNCTAD had an unambiguous mandate in the UN system for ECDC, with an ECDC Division and a Members' Committee, and UNCTAD provided comprehensive recommendations for action and approval by the conference. These included the establishment of a global system of trade preferences among developing countries (GSTP), of state trading organizations (STOS) as a counter to TNCS, of multinational marketing enterprises, producer associations, and financial institutions. UNCTAD also asked for additional support to meet its increased responsibilities.[84]

The UNCTAD secretariat proposals were supplemented by the Arusha Declaration (see discussion in Chapter 3 of the Plan for Collective Self-Reliance), which proposed a series of UNCTAD-staffed meetings to be held by the end of 1979.[85] The ministers also urged the DCS to "abandon their negative attitudes" and to support the program, called on the United Nations and the United Nations Development Program (UNDP) to intensify support for ECDC, and advised the LDCs to draw up shopping lists for presentation to the DCS and the UNDP.[86]

The United States and other Group B countries have generally supported the idea of ECDC. They have had some reservations (trend toward autarky, questionable feasibility of some of the proposals, discrimination against DC commerce and industry, and more bureaucratic empire building), but none of them were overriding. What concerned those countries the most was the G-77 using UNCTAD for exclusive LDC purposes. They have maintained, quite rightly, that UNCTAD is a common UN organization and should keep at least the pretense of universality. They were afraid that the DCS would not only have to pay for the meetings but would have to agree to programs in which they had had no say. The LDCs would thus have succeeded in circumventing the TDB.[87] That problem lies behind the Arusha complaint about the "DCS' negative attitude," and, typically, the problem figured as the central issue at UNCTAD V.

Nevertheless, the G-77 countries got pretty much what they were after—a program of work based on the Mexico City program, liberal support commitments from the DCS and international organizations, an endorsement of UNCTAD's support capabilities, and agreement to the suggested series of meetings, including "exclusive" LDC meetings.[88] But the G-77 did not achieve those goals easily. The negotiations were long and difficult. Group B raised serious questions about UNCTAD's role in ECDC and its responsibilities within the UN system, the lack of priorities in the proposed work program, and exclusive meetings among the LDCs. Group B finally agreed to a special session of the full ECDC committee, preceded by three LDC experts' meetings and other meetings of LDC regional groups that were to be seen as an extension of the system of "group caucuses" on an ad hoc basis.

According to the UNCTAD legal adviser, such meetings would not "stretch the UNCTAD rule of universality any further than it had already been stretched by the caucus system." With regard to the program, Group B had great difficulty in accepting a program that was based strictly on Arusha, which would give a "blank-check endorsement for the results of a meeting they did not attend."[89] Nevertheless, the United States was satisfied with the final resolution, which recognized the principle of universality in UN bodies. The G-77 resolution would have limited participation at the 1980 meeting of the ECDC committee to only the G-77.

The Least Developed Countries (LLDCs)

Assistance to the LLDCs had nothing to do with the NIEO, predated it, and was not even mentioned in the declaration. It is included here because it was on the UNCTAD V agenda, because of its intrinsic interest, and because of its influence on the North-South dialogue. Like energy, assistance to the LLDCs is a "wild card," but in this case it is essential to the advanced LDCs because they need the support of the many LLDCs on items of interest to them, e.g., the transfer of technology. For the United States, with its basic needs policy, such assistance has a direct and an unambiguous importance. Therefore, although LDCs may reject "basic needs," they cannot reject aid to the LLDCs; North and South are agreed on at least one thing, if for different reasons.

The plight of the world's poorest peoples has become an international cause célèbre, involving a variously estimated 800 million people, mostly in sub-Saharan Africa and South Asia, who still live in absolute poverty. They have become the focus of the World Bank's program and of the U.S. bilateral aid program. Former Secretary Kissinger, in his speech to the Seventh Special Session of the General Assembly in September 1975, said: "Whatever adversity the rest of mankind endures, it is these peoples who endure the most. Whatever problems we have, theirs are monumental. . . . No international order can be considered just unless one of its fundamental principles is cooperation to raise the poorest of the world to a decent stan- dard of life."[90]

All of the LLDCs suffer from some serious obstacle to development — e.g., extreme poverty, lack of natural resources, geographical disadvan- tage — and special measures are required of overcome those obstacles.

Nevertheless, the efforts of the seventies failed to have much effect. According to UNCTAD, the economic growth of the LLDCs as a whole stagnated and, in some areas, actually declined from the levels of the sixties.[91]

UNCTAD called for the conference to launch a two-phase action program for the eighties. Phase 1 called for massive transfers and training on an emergency basis, and Phase 2 was to be a longer-range program to overcome structural weaknesses, climatic handicaps, and physical constraints, e.g., remoteness and "landlockedness." The program recommended a tripling of aid flows, new studies by UNCTAD, a high-level group of experts, and a special UN conference on the least developed countries to launch the program and to generate pledges to the program. Primary responsibility for the program was to be held by UNCTAD.[92]

The Arusha Programme repeated the UNCTAD proposals verbatim, except that UNCTAD's recommendations for LDC assistance were cut back from half a page to one sentence and demands on the DCs were spelled out in detail and at twice the length. Those demands included a doubling of ODA by 1981, a crash emergency program, special consideration for LLDCs on all aspects of trade and aid, and various means to expand UNCTAD operations and staff.[93]

The United States gave the resolution on the least developed countries its full support, with certain strategic reservations. U.S. policy, as noted, strongly favored increased assistance to the least developed countries, RTA, liberalized concessional aid, and taking the LLDCs into special account in the MTNs. However, as with the transfer of technology, the United States disagreed with the G-77/UNCTAD perspective, which put emphasis on externalities rather than on appropriate internal policies to make the external aid effective. Nor would the United States accept any rigid quotas on ODA increases. It did support the action plan, provided the plan "judiciously distributed the obligations among DCs, LDCs and international institutions."[94]

The conference passed a resolution at the last moment that provided for a Comprehensive New Program of Action. The resolution included an oblique reference to basic needs ("social objectives"), toned down the call for a "crash program" to a call for "immediate action," and substituted "as soon as possible" for "doubling aid in three years."[95] The United States was satisfied with the final result because the resolution moved in the direction of U.S. policy, which has tried for years to focus UNCTAD and the North-South dialogue on the poorest countries, and because the international community, not just the DCs, was involved in the effort. At the final plenary session, the United States made the usual reservations concerning ODA commitments but noted that the United States expected to increase aid to the least developed countries over the "near term" and stressed the great importance the United States attaches to the integration of the New Program into the International Development Strategy for the 1980s.[96]

Summary

Fortunately, I am not obliged to determine whether UNCTAD V was a "success" or a "failure," the principal question hanging over any conference. Suffice to say, opinions are mixed, and those countries with the highest expectations or hopes—the G-77—were the most disillusioned and disappointed. My only concern has been to discover what went on at the negotiating table on the premise that the reality of the North-South dialogue is what happens at the actual negotiations and that studying what occurred during negotiations makes the reasons for cooperation or opposition understandable. That is to say, general subjects—e.g., technology transfer or increased resource transfers—usually look quite different when they are broken down to specific components of personnel, funding, and program. Thus, a General Assembly resolution that is addressed to a general objective and is supported by a consensus can, and obviously does, bog down at the negotiating table when the specifics have to be hammered out. Furthermore, during the negotiations, specific proposals become bargaining chips, which may or may not make it through the negotiating process whatever their intrinsic merit.

Interdependence

The United States would have supported a resolution on interdependence, but not on G-77 terms. The U.S. delegation rejected the claim that a NIEO was necessary on the grounds that the current economic order was flexible and was adapting to new needs, including those of the LDCs, and that structural adjustment was occurring, with the free-market system acting as an efficient arbitrator.

With regard to development, per se, the United States believed that the critical factors were internal ones—meeting basic needs—not external ones. The object of development is not resource transfers but an improvement in the lives of people. The United States opposed new institutional approaches such as the establishment of a new high-level advisory group to conduct global consultations, which, the United States believed, was unnecessary, would duplicate the COW, and would infringe on the responsibilities of the IMF, IBRD, and GATT.

The United States would not agree to any resolution on interdependence that did not include energy, since energy is at the heart of the matter. The LDCs suspected that the United States was "playing the energy card" to split the Third World, and their suspicion was not without some foundation. However, the gravity of the issue was such that the United States would have insisted on including energy, whatever the position of the non-oil-exporting LDCS.

Trade

The United States took a positive stand on protectionism, which it is trying to resist domestically and worldwide. The main U.S. interest in a trade resolution was largely its desire to get the commitment of all countries, North and South. But the United States balked at the G-77 concept that governments should be the driving force behind an adjustment process and that UNCTAD should be given the central role in protectionism and adjustment. The United States believed that adjustment should be a response to market forces, not to government direction. The United States was willing to "facilitate" change but not to legislate it.

The United States sought to gain endorsement of the MTNs, maintaining that the Tokyo Round had been moderately successful and had taken LDC needs and interests fully into account. The G-77 sought to reopen the negotiations under UNCTAD auspices and recommended a new trading system with UNCTAD at the center. No DC, let alone the United States, would consider for a moment reopening the Tokyo Round negotiations or relinquishing the GATT system for an UNCTAD-managed trading system.

The United States has been opposed from the beginning to a "managed" commodity system or to any arrangement that would increase the independent power of LDC producers, and the United States maintained its opposition in UNCTAD V. Concerning the IPC, the United States was already committed to negotiations on individual commodity agreements but resisted efforts to force the pace through an arbitrary UNCTAD timetable on the grounds that there was still too much technical work to be done before meaningful negotiations could take place. The United States opposed a "comprehensive framework" under UNCTAD direction to promote processing in LDCs, on the grounds that it was better not to legislate objectives but to let market forces dictate changes according to economic realities, and it opposed a new, costly, and probably redundant facility for compensatory finance. The United States also opposed any increase in UNCTAD programs or any intrusion by UNCTAD into the responsibilities of other organizations. In short, the commodities issue was mainly one of the LDCs supporting a more managed, UNCTAD-centered system that would replace the existing free market system and its institutions.

The issue on manufacture and semimanufacture was between another "comprehensive strategy" (including the usual paraphernalia of targets, managed structural adjustments, control of the TNCs, and more technical aid within a system of global consultations and an international policy framework) on the one hand and, on the other, Group B adherence to a market-oriented system in which no country is permanently relieved of the obligation of nondiscriminatory reciprocity and in which the LDCs should gradually assume increasing responsibility as economic progress permits. The DCs had made serious commitments to international adjustment, but that was as a matter of internal policy and was not subject to international direction or control.

The United States and Group B generally have had a long-standing interest in repressing RBPs and have been well ahead of the G-77 in formulating their own international "guidelines." Where the United States disagrees with the G-77 is in the setting up of international machinery under UNCTAD to manage or monitor RBPs and in putting the RBP guidelines on a legal or mandatory basis.

The United States also wanted a resolution on the GSP that would make, at most, a moral commitment to the continuation of and an improvement in the GSP system. The G-77, however, wanted a commitment to binding GSP benefits and to negotiating the GSP under UNCTAD. These demands were not acceptable to the DCs on the grounds that the GSP is a unilateral concession and therefore is nonnegotiable.

Monetary and Financial Issues

As far as the United States was concerned, the international monetary system was nonnegotiable, at least in UNCTAD. It therefore rejected the idea that decisions on monetary issues could take place outside of the IMF, the call for a high-level group of experts in UNCTAD, the need for a special balance-of-payments facility, and G-77 proposals that would erode the monetary nature of the IMF by skewing it toward development objectives.

Concerning resource transfers, the United States had nothing to offer and nothing to ask. It opposed every G-77 initiative for commitments to increasing resource transfers and rejected international targets for volume or terms of ODA. With regard to private finance, the United States could not and would not interfere in capital markets, so it could not endorse the idea of massive transfers. It opposed the creation of an export credit guarantee facility (ECGF) because it would be a low-priority use of scarce resources and because of a reluctance to tamper with international capital markets.

With regard to debt, the United States has adopted the policy of RTA but has opposed across-the-board debt cancellation, because serious indebtedness is not that widespread a problem and such cancellation would violate the international system and set an unmanageable precedent. The United States opposed setting up a debt commission, any threat to creditor group integrity, and any increased UNCTAD role in the debt area.

Under the heading of "International Financial Cooperation," the G-77 proposed setting up a "complementary" system to do what the present system could not do, they said, including establishing a "multilateral framework," a new international fund for trade and development (IFTD), and a high-level group of experts, presumably under UNCTAD auspices. The United States opposed all those ideas or proposals on the grounds that the present system was sufficiently diversified to meet all needs, the competence of the international institutions should not be impaired, and it was important to respect free initiative and to preserve the flexibility of private capital markets and operations.

Transfer of Technology

The United States favors a code of conduct for the transfer of technology but adamantly opposes any attempt to make one mandatory. The code should stimulate, not legislate, and a mandatory code would be unworkable and tend to inhibit the very reason for having a code. The United States resisted any effort to give UNCTAD a role in WIPO's Geneva conference in 1980 for revising the Paris Convention for the Protection of Industrial Property but favored and has supported a revised convention that takes LDC interests and problems fully into account.

The United States strongly favors an increased LDC technology capacity but has opposed setting up an international fund, an open-ended mandate for UNCTAD (including increased staff and program), or a comprehensive global strategy. In regard to the brain drain, the United States has opposed UNCTAD involvement and, especially, any idea of a labor compensatory scheme.

In summary, on the technology items, the United States saw the main issues at UNCTAD V as being centered on the institutional role of UNCTAD. These issues included the legal nature of the code of conduct, interference in the WIPO negotiations, a new UNCTAD Secretariat program on the transfer of technology, a new fund, a comprehensive global strategy, and an UNCTAD mandate on the labor compensatory scheme — all of which the United States opposed.

Economic Cooperation Among Developing Countries

The United States generally favored programs in support of ECDC and agreed to the Action Plan and to UNCTAD's central role. But the United States opposed using UNCTAD as an exclusive LDC club, with exclusive LDC meetings, and UNCTAD's encroaching on the responsibilities of other UN agencies. U.S. support in this area does not imply any support of the NIEO, although the G-77 made explicit reference to the close relationship between ECDC and the NIEO.

The Least Developed Countries

The United States was forthcoming on aid to the least developed countries because it directly supports the basic needs concept. The United States therefore went along, albeit reluctantly, with the UNCTAD V resolution for the Comprehensive New Program of Action, a special UN conference, and strengthening UNCTAD facilities.

Conclusions

The general U.S. objective at UNCTAD V was to obtain international commitments to reduce protectionism and to promote adjustment and to "focus" UNCTAD V on food, the very poor, energy, and technology — i.e., along the lines of U.S. interests and priorities as outlined by Secretary Vance in his March 30, 1979, speech in Seattle. Toward those ends, the United States supported a consensus on "interdependence," including the recognition of energy as an issue (which failed); a consensus on rights and responsibilities as they concern protectionism and the need for industrial adjustment; trade concessions for the LDCs (MTNs and the GSP); elimination of RBPs; gradual improvement in the international monetary system; debt relief as RTA, not cancellation; a voluntary code of conduct on the transfer of technology; recognition of LDC interests in the renegotiation of the Paris Convention on industrial property; increased aid to the least developed countries; and improved ECDC.

On the other hand, the United States opposed

1. the creation of any new institutions: e.g., a new compensatory finance facility, a special balance-of-payments facility, an export credit guarantee facility (ECGF), a debt commission, an international fund for trade and development (IFTD), a fund for technological transfer, and a labor compensatory scheme.
2. any significant expansion of UNCTAD responsibilities: e.g., a central role for UNCTAD in monetary or adjustment policies and the organization of adjustment "negotiations"; reopening the MTNs under UNCTAD auspices; placing UNCTAD at the center of a new trading system; increasing UNCTAD authority and programs in the area of commodities (processing, marketing, and distribution); UNCTAD machinery for reviewing RBPs; negotiations on the GSP in UNCTAD; a high-level group of experts on monetary reform, debt policy, and management; international financial cooperation; negotiations on industrial property (WIPO); an open-ended UNCTAD mandate on technological transfer; and responsibilities in the reverse transfer of technology.

3. any extension of international management and planning: e.g., governments being the "driving force" behind adjustment, including the negotiation of adjustment issues; a comprehensive framework for production and marketing in the commodities area; a comprehensive strategy for managing changes in manufacturing, adjustment, and processing; a legal code for RBPS and a mandatory code for the transfer of technology; a multilateral framework for international financial cooperation, including a high-level group of experts; a comprehensive global strategy for technological transfer; and a comprehensive program for action for the least developed countries.

4. any financial commitments to new UNCTAD programs, funds, or institutions or any commitment to target levels or arbitrary amounts of aid or financial transfers through the capital market.

5. any erosion of the existing international system, including UNCTAD intrusion into the responsibilities of other agencies; any threat to U.S. autonomy, e.g., commitments to ODA levels; negotiation of the GSP or international negotiation of adjustment; any extension of international authority over the private sector, e.g., the production, marketing, and finance of commodities; interference in capital markets and so-called international financial cooperation; any threat to the authority of the IMF or to the policies and management of the MDBs; and any interference in creditor group authority.

Not only did the United States oppose the above features, all of which appeared in the UNCTAD documentation, in the Arusha Declaration or both, the United States demonstrated that much of the agenda was nonnegotiable: the monetary system, the Tokyo Round, the present GATT-centered trading system, the GSP, ODA levels, international management of any sort beyond the present institutions, any substantial increase in UNCTAD's role and authority, and financial commitments. The specifics varied from issue to issue, but the policy remained the same: no funds, no institutions, no expansion of UNCTAD, no change in the present system, no impairment of U.S. autonomy, no increased international management, no invasion of the private sector. In other words, the United States, although supporting most of the ultimate objectives of Third World development, rejected the means and methods by which the G-77 sought to bring those changes about: international management, new institutions, erosion of the present institutions, an increase of UNCTAD authority, increased bureaucracy, increased costs at the management level, interference with the free-market economy.

Thus, on the negotiating level, the real differences over the NIEO do become apparent, and those differences are not so much differences over economic or social objectives as over the international system—how it works, who pays for it, who takes the risks, who benefits, and, above all, who controls it. It is clear that, au fond, the NIEO is a political matter—which should come as no surprise to the Non-Aligned.

Summer 1979: Full Circle

UNCTAD V finally collapsed in exhaustion in the early hours of June 3. Except for a spate of post mortems, all bad, the North turned hastily to other things and put UNCTAD V, the North-South dialogue, the Third World, and international social and economic rearrangement behind it. Delegates took home their papers, wrote their reports, and sent the lot to the file rooms. During the quiet summer months that followed, it seemed as if nothing had happened or was happening.

But the quiet was deceptive, and the months following the Manila meeting were probably more important for the North-South dialogue than anything that had happened at UNCTAD V. The single major conference was replaced by a succession of events and issues, including two world conferences — one in Rome and the other in Vienna — to which the world paid no attention whatsoever. The first was the World Conference on Agrarian Reform and Rural Development (WCARRD), sponsored by the Food and Agriculture Organization (FAO) and held in Rome in July 1979, and the second was the UN Conference on Science and Technology for Development (UNCSTD) held in Vienna in August. Both had taken years to prepare for, both addressed vital issues, both were reasonably successful, and both were ignored by the press and caught the conscience of the world napping — or, more probably, at the beach.

The Uninvited Guest: Oil

Besides food and technology, there was a third issue, energy, that could not be ignored. The energy issue had disrupted UNCTAD V, lingering in the corridors like an uninvited guest. Ultimately, it became the force that propelled the North-South dialogue beyond the stagnation of Manila toward a whole new generation of negotiations that began in the summer of 1980.

Although not on the UNCTAD V agenda and deliberately suppressed to maintain Third World unity, the energy problem had walked in the door when UN Secretary-General Waldheim, speaking at the opening session on

May 7, cited food and energy as crucial development problems and called
for a common effort by all nations if the adjustment to new energy sources
were not to have adverse effects on the process of development.[1] U.S. Ambassador Andrew Young, in his May 11 speech to the plenary session,
flagged oil prices as one of the main problems of the LDCs, charging that
"global development had been seriously retarded" both because of the direct
impact on the LDCs and because of the slowing of world economic growth.
The heaviest burden, he pointed out, had "with cruel irony often fallen on
the most underdeveloped countries who are least able to bear it."[2] Young's
remarks were the opening shot of a U.S. guerrilla campaign throughout
UNCTAD V that associated the energy problem with the other basic problems of food, population, education, and health that afflict the poorest
countries.

On Monday May 14, Dr. Alfonso Rudes, head of the Colombian delegation, let the cat out of the LDC bag by protesting in a plenary session against
the severe hardship caused by the oil price increases and demanding that oil
be brought within UNCTAD's mandate.[3] The energy issue erupted shortly
thereafter in the negotiating group on interdependence, and that group's
resolution became the first casualty of the conference. Group B was determined to keep an energy section in the resolution and urged "all member
countries to take appropriate steps to improve the balance of supply and demand for energy . . . noting in particular the needs of the non-oil-devel-
oping countries,[4] but the G-77 draft resolution contained no references to
energy. Many Latin American delegates wanted to see the negotiations collapse to make the point that without energy on the agenda, global negotiations could not take place. On the other hand, it was rumored that Idriss
Jazairy (Algeria) would have preferred that the negotiations collapse rather
than have the discussion lead to energy. Venezuela, a member of both the
Latin American group (Group C) and OPEC, was caught in the middle and
tried to play a mediating role, promising that OPEC would take up development and energy as a topic at the OPEC ministerial meeting in late June.[5]

The United States kept the pressure on to the end. On May 28, it released a special study prepared for the conference as a delegation
background paper on oil. That study showed that at present prices, non-
OPEC LDCs would face a $5-billion increase in their aggregate 1979 trade
deficits, resulting directly and indirectly from the 24 percent increase in oil
prices to that point in 1979, and that their current account deficits would
rise from $28 billion to $37 billion. Meanwhile, the current account
surpluses of the OPEC member countries would rise to at least $29 billion,
twenty times the 1978 level.[6]

In a parting shot, U.S. Delegate Charles Meissner used his end-of-
conference statement to the press to cite disagreement among the develop-

ing countries as the major obstacle to the deliberations on interdependence. He reiterated the U.S. and Group B position that it was unrealistic, at a conference devoted to trade and development, to ignore the question of energy. However, he said, the conference was unable to deal with the question because the OPEC countries were opposed to any such discussion in UNCTAD.[7]

After UNCTAD V, the energy issue was out in the open, and it was impossible to suppress it any longer. The final communiqué of the Non-Aligned Coordinating Bureau, which met in Colombo in June, stated that energy must be discussed in the context of global negotiations. The communiqué noted the possibility of a positive decision being made at the forthcoming Non-Aligned Summit in Havana.

OPEC, as promised by Venezuela at UNCTAD V, did take up both energy and development at its ministerial meeting in Geneva on June 26. Its June 28 communiqué began with the good news.[8] The conference expressed concern for the problems being faced by the developing countries, "especially in the light of continued lack of readiness on the part of the industrialized countries to face up to their responsibilities toward the problems of the Third World." The OPEC countries, having already "proved their solidarity with the Third World" and having already contributed in many ways to "alleviate the problems of other developing countries," would add another $800 million to the Arab Development Fund and undertake further study of a long-term finance facility.

The communiqué then responded to what it said had been proposals for a dialogue between OPEC and the industrialized countries. Although OPEC would be willing to discuss energy, it categorically rejected any dialogue that did not also take into account the problems of "development, and acquisition of advanced technology, financial and monetary reforms, world trade and raw materials, along with the various aspects of the energy problem." That was OPEC's signal to the OECD countries that oil negotiations would have a price tag, both economic and political; that the path to agreement in 1979, as in 1974, had to be negotiated; and that the issue had to be negotiated on a broad front.

Then came the bad news, as if to drive home the point. "In an endeavor to bring some stability to the market, the conference decided on the following: to adjust the market crude price from the present level to $18 a barrel; to allow members to add . . . a maximum market premium of $2 a barrel . . . ; and that the maximum price . . . shall not exceed $23.50 a barrel."

Tokyo: The Energy Summit

The fifth summit of the "big seven"[9] convened in Tokyo on June 28,

1979, the day OPEC issued its communiqué. "This time," one U.S. administration official said, "all the delegates will be on one side of the table and the problem of energy will be on the other side."[10]

Preceding Tokyo had been six months of oil price increases. During December 1978, OPEC members had begun to add surcharges to the official price of $13.34 a barrel. In March 1979, the official price had been set at $14.55, with new surcharges of up to $7 to follow. On June 28, as we have seen, OPEC had announced a new floor price of $18 and a permitted maximum of $23.50. Before long, several OPEC members were to break through that ceiling to start a two-tier OPEC pricing system and, within OPEC, a tug-of-war between moderates like Saudi Arabia and radicals like Libya.

On June 1, 1979, the OECD semiannual forecast had made gloomy reading. Economic growth, it had predicted, would slow to 3.4 percent in 1979, down from 3.7 percent in 1978, the worst slowdown since the 1974–1975 recession. The OECD had also predicted for the next twelve months an average economic growth of 2 percent, a rise in the inflation rate from 7.9 percent to 10 percent, and a rise in unemployment from 5.25 percent to 6 percent—to a postwar record of 19 million people out of work in OECD countries. Balance-of-payments deficits would double to $40 billion. The OECD's advice to policymakers had been to "sit tight" and reduce oil imports.[11]

As usual, the United States was the center of contention, and with good reason. For months, resentment in Europe and the rest of the world had been growing over the United States' inability or unwillingness to curb its oil consumption. President of France Valéry Giscard d'Estaing and West German Chancellor Helmut Schmidt, greatly unimpressed by Carter's performance, turned toward increased European cooperation and a more "independent" line. Third World resentments were directed more toward the United States than toward OPEC as seemingly insatiable U.S. consumption kept prices rising, the LDC debt escalating, and development inexorably slowing down. Within the United States, competing demands for the scarce oil set region against region, producer against consumer, industry against transportation. The result? A consensus on how to deal with energy was impossible to achieve.

The role of the dollar was becoming more questionable than ever. The international economic and monetary system was already glutted with petrodollars, and there was growing doubt that it could effectively recycle them any longer. With the dollar weakening, the big dollar holders were making a frantic search for ways to hedge against loss by investing in currency "baskets," gold, land, and industry.

President Carter's political stock, already falling for some time, was being driven down even further. Europeans complained about his apparent lack of authority and leadership; Americans tended to agree, and Congress refused to cooperate with Carter in trying to resolve any of the outstanding problems. With the prospect that SALT II (signed in Vienna just a few days before the Tokyo Summit) would get mauled in the U.S. Senate and with an election year just around the corner (with all of its political consequences), Jimmy Carter was in a tough spot.

The summit members met the energy issue head on, stressing the damage that was being done to both DCs and LDCs,[12] and said that the most urgent tasks were to reduce consumption and to hasten the development of alternative energy sources. The member countries pledged to restrict 1979 oil consumption by specified amounts and to maintain imports through 1985 at levels no higher than the levels of 1979 (10 million barrels per day for the EC, 8.5 million barrels per day for the United States, and between 6.3 million and 6.9 million barrels per day for Japan). Meanwhile, the leaders would seek to increase coal production and trade, and to expand alternative sources of energy, including nuclear energy. Returning OPEC's fire, the summit members "deplored" the OPEC decision to raise prices again, which meant "more world-wide inflation, less growth, more unemployment, more balance-of-payment difficulties and more damage to stability in developing and developed countries alike."[13]

Constructive North-South relations were seen as being essential to the health of the world economy. The members had worked hard to bring the LDCs into the "open world trading system and to adjust our economies to changing international circumstances,"[14] but the partnership could not depend solely on the efforts of the industrial countries. The OPEC countries must play just as important a role. The latest price increases would not only hurt the LDCs but make it more difficult for the DCs to help them. The summit members emphasized their concern for the millions of people living in absolute poverty and promised to urge multinational organizations to help those countries develop effective food sector strategies, storage capacities for strong national food reserves, and increased R&D for agriculture and energy. Finally, the Tokyo delegates declared, "we are ready to examine with oil exporting countries how to define supply and demand prospects on the world market," a hedged reply to the OPEC offer to negotiate.[15]

Jimmy Carter came back from Tokyo a troubled man. The nation — shocked by the Iranian revolution, angered by the new OPEC price increase, beginning to realize in a dim way that the energy crunch was real and not contrived — waited for his promised report to the nation on the well-publicized Tokyo Summit. Instead, the president cancelled his speech without explanation and went into near seclusion at Camp David. It was a dramatic move, mysterious and seemingly impetuous, and it whetted the country's interest even further. Days passed, high-level visitors came and went, but no announcements were forthcoming. Some people speculated that his silence was political dramatics.

Finally, nearly two weeks later, Carter spoke to the nation. He had obviously been agonizing, not just over economic problems, but over the United States. The country, he said, was suffering from a spiritual malaise; it had lost touch with itself, and the time had come to return to the basics — to God, country, and family. Having thus set the mood, he laid down the main features of a proposed program to respond realistically to the mounting energy problem. The United States had reached the limit of its imports, he declared; from that day forward it would never, repeat never, import more oil than it was now doing. There followed a list of tough new proposals for a windfall profits tax, a national energy administration, and a research and development program for alternative energy resources, which, he declared, would have to be adopted if the country were to survive. A week later he stunned the country by firing some of his top cabinet members. To many Europeans, unfamiliar with the U.S. system, it seemed that the government had fallen. Among those tapped to go were Attorney General Griffin Bell, Energy Secretary James Schlesinger, and Treasury Secretary W. Michael Blumenthal.

This was the new "tough" Carter, showing the world that he meant business and that he was, indeed, very much in charge of the government. The Europeans were not, however, impressed; they were puzzled, mistrusted Carter's moralizing, and were skeptical of grand pronouncements. Carter had not mentioned the all important decontrol of U.S. crude oil prices and had made no mention of nuclear energy. The dollar continued to waver, and the price of gold continued to increase. In short, rightly or wrongly, there was a vast vote of no confidence abroad. But Americans did not take the speech so lightly, and for the moment at least, they agreed with the president. Congress suddenly found itself awash with energy bills. There was clearly a new mood in the country that was a change from the inertia and confusion of the preceding months, the first sign that the head-in-the-sand, post-Vietnam attitude might be changing. In his farewell speech at the National Press Club on August 16, Energy Secretary Schlesinger painted an even grimmer picture than the president had. Combining the elements of Middle East political instability, Soviet ambition, and the U.S. dependence on Middle East oil, Schlesinger declared that "we face a world crisis of vaster dimensions than Churchill described a half century ago," which could mean "the end of the world as we have known it since 1945 and of the association of free nations."[16]

Remote though these matters and events may seem to have been from the immediate concerns of the North-South dialogue or the NIEO, they were very much in the mainstream of both. The fortunes of the dialogue and of the developing nations—indeed, of the whole world, North and South—depended, ultimately, on what success the United States had in coming to grips with its energy problems, both in the near and in the long term. UNC-TAD V, if it served no other purpose, did force the energy issue and its effects on development to the surface. Sheikh Yamani underlined the significance of the energy link in a speech on January 7, 1980, to a symposium of international businessmen in Davos, Switzerland. He warned that OPEC production rates would be cut back unless the West offered technology rather than depreciating currency, that OPEC would not discuss the price of oil in isolation. What was needed, he said, was a comprehensive Third World strategy for financial contributions by the industrialized world to develop Third World resources.[17]

World Conference on Agrarian Reform and Rural Development (WCARRD)

While Carter was agonizing over energy, the World Conference on Agrarian Reform and Rural Development (WCARRD) met in Rome from July 12 to July 20 under FAO auspices to draw up a program on a question that was most crucial to the LDCs and especially the poorest countries: rural development and agrarian reform. It is to be regretted that the conference was overshadowed by the problems of the industrialized world, for not only did it address the basic and ticklish problem of agrarian reform but was successful in a way that UNCTAD V would have liked to have been. Single-issue conferences usually are successful, and sometimes quiet obscurity is the key. But the conference's achievements should not have been lost in the summer doldrums, for WCARRD met to take international action on the very problem about which the developed world at Tokyo said it was the most concerned—the millions of the poorest peoples—and to provide the substantive programs without which the northern concerns would be empty rhetoric.

"Rural poverty is now recognized as the biggest problem of the world development struggle," said Chilean Ambassador Hernan Santa Cruz, special representative of the FAO director-general for WCARRD. Although the green revolution is important, the root causes of rural poverty lie deeper in obsolete agrarian structures, imbalanced development strategies, and unjust international systems.[18]

The numbers are daunting. Nearly half of the world's population of 4 billion lives in the rural areas of developing countries. More than half of those people are poor, and three-quarters of the poor live in absolute destitution. And the numbers are growing. Despite migration to the cities, a huge problem in itself, the rural population of the LDCs is expected to grow by almost another billion before the turn of the century, with the sons and daughters of today's small farmers and agricultural workers accounting for most of that increase.[19]

The object of the conference, therefore, was to set up a cooperative program for change and development that addressed the real obstacles to change and in the right way. These obstacles were (1) an inequitable distribution of land and water, (2) the emergence of a rural proletariat, (3) the fact that modernization had passed the small farmer by, (4) widespread tenant farming and sharecropping and the abuse of fair rent laws, and (5) the inability of governments to deliver services to small farmers. All these problems could be alleviated by purposeful government action. The conference would also examine the relationship between rural development and the international system, especially the terms of trade for agricultural commodities. The internal savings that are required to effect reform cannot be made without "fairer" prices for exports and better access to DC markets.[20] The agenda nicely provided for conflict between the two classic perspectives of basic needs and the NIEO, which are never far from confrontation.

U.S. policy was that it was "in the U.S. national interest to ensure a positive and constructive outcome for WCARRD." The United States had identified four North-South objectives that it would support over the long term: (1) alleviation of the worst physical aspects of poverty, (2) promotion of self-sustaining "growth with equity," (3) encouragement of societies that value individual civil and economic rights, and (4) integration of LDCs into an "open and equitable international economic system." It was believed that WCARRD would advance all four objectives. Within them, the U.S. government wished to concentrate on five priority areas: energy, food, health, LDC capacity for development, and institutional reforms.[21]

With regard to the "international system," the United States would discuss policy questions relevant to agrarian reform but emphasize, if necessary, that the broader aspects of those questions have been under discussion in UNCTAD, the MTNs, the COW, etc. The U.S. delegation was instructed to ensure that no new international institutions or new special funds for rural development were created by WCARRD.[22] It was expected that the United States ought to "come out of this conference with an enhanced and positive image in the eyes of the Third World" and that that image would have an important "carry-over impact" at UNCSTD and UNIDO III.[23]

In spite of the likelihood of confrontation, the conference adopted a Declaration of Principles and a Program of Action with few (though important) reservations. Commission 1 adopted an Agenda of National Policies for Agrarian Reform and Rural Development without major disagreement.

The agenda retained an emphasis on "growth with equity," and all delegations except Argentina's acknowledged the need to increase equity and to move toward a redistribution of wealth (land) and power as an essential condition to successful and overall development, to establish clear targets, and to monitor progress. The United States reserved agreement on government acquisition of natural resources when the commission rejected language that made such acquisition consistent with international law and added the CERDS text for good measure.[24]

In Commission 2, which became a mini–UNCTAD V, North-South differences quickly surfaced, and agrarian reform was rarely even mentioned. Most DCS took the position that they were not prepared to negotiate their positions on trade, development assistance, and foreign investment at WCARRD. They noted that UNCTAD V had just concluded and that they had not changed their positions since that conference. Compensation for expropriation emerged as the most contentious item. The host of differences on that and other items — trade and ODA, for example — resulted in a G-77 text with multiple DC reservations that essentially repeated the recommendations of UNCTAD V.[25]

The Preamble and Declaration of Principles were to be drawn up by a joint session of the two commissions, and confrontation was avoided only by the skillful work of the UK representative, Dame Judith Hart, who acted as chairman. The conflict between the basic needs and NIEO concepts was "worked out" in the sixteen preambular paragraphs. And, although the Preamble represented a G-77 notice board more than a policy statement, it did achieve the remarkable feat of accommodating both points of view in one statement. The operational paragraph seems to be paragraph 8, in which the requirements for agrarian reform and rural development were viewed "in the context of promotion of national self-reliance and building of the NIEO."[26] In other words, basic needs became a means to an end, the inverse of the U.S. perspective, which regarded international measures as a means to meeting basic needs.

Considering the pitfalls into which the conference might have fallen, the G-77 mood of frustration following UNCTAD V, and the unfolding of later events, it was a wonder that WCARRD did as well as it did. Considerable credit has been given to the FAO and its Director-General Edouard Saouma's handling of the conference, not to mention the good work of Dame Judith Hart. Saouma kept the conference short and the organization simple, preconference consultations were limited to one meeting of a preparatory group, the meeting was closely orchestrated by top experts, and there was a special representative (Santa Cruz) to make things go.

Nevertheless, one cannot escape the feeling that the conference was "passed over" as a strategic occasion to be used to push hard for southern interests. There were no demands for new funds or organizations, and the accommodation of heretofore conflicting views was "easily" achieved. Expected political issues — e.g., the Palestine Liberation Organization (PLO), Cambodia, Israel — did not emerge. There were no walkouts by the Soviets, the Africans, or the Arabs as there had been at UNCTAD V. The conference was suspiciously quiet.

The U.S. position also remained something of a mystery. WCARRD, at least Commission 1, provided an international endorsement of the programs that were of greatest concern to the U.S. development effort, and yet the United States was a reluctant participant. It did not advocate calling the conference during the debate in the FAO in 1977, it "finally went along . . . hoping that some tangible and useful results would emerge,"[27] and it sent a small and undistinguished delegation while some countries — Senegal, Bangladesh, and Tanzania — sent heads of state. The official who was primarily responsible for coordinating the U.S. participation stated that it had been difficult to get a "liberal and forthcoming position because everything impinging on land reform was covered by U.S. positions on the NIEO." The State Department's Bureau of Economic and Business Affairs (EB) was the main stumbling block, as it was "primarily concerned with short-range problems and solutions."[28]

On the surface, it would appear that the United States had missed an opportunity. But the fact that "growth with equity"[29] and basic needs are fundamental U.S. policies would suggest that there were "other reasons" for the United States' low profile at WCARRD — possibly it was because of a desire not to "internationalize" a bilateral program or perhaps it was a vote of no confidence in the FAO or Director-General Saouma. The U.S. delegation's instructions had been specific: the United States would provide support, but through its bilateral programs and the MDBS.[30]

UN Conference on Science and Technology for Development (UNCSTD)

A month after WCARRD, on August 20, the last of the UN megaconferences of the seventies, UNCSTD, brought together 4,000 delegates from 150 countries in Vienna at an estimated cost of $50 million for an eleven-day conference. It was the culmination of years of thought if not of action. A predecessor (the West's answer to Sputnik) had met in 1963 in Geneva and produced a UN Advisory Committee for the Application of Science and Technology for Development (ACAST), a staff, and a world plan of action, but little else.[31] The Sixth Special Session had highlighted science and technology needs in the declaration on the NIEO, and the Seventh Special Session had called for a world conference.

UNCSTD's purpose was to draw up an action plan for the application of science and technology (S&T) to Third World needs to overcome the disparity caused by only 3 percent of the world's R&D budget being spent on Third World problems. To achieve that aim, the conference would work (1) to strengthen the developing world's S&T capabilities, (2) to determine ways to accelerate economic and social development through S&T, and (3) to create and strengthen the appropriate mechanisms of international cooperation for these purposes. Thus, the conference was to be primarily concerned with how to acquire S&T and how to put it to use in meeting the needs of the developing countries.

But the conference was beset by conflict from the beginning, and its focus was distorted in many ways by political strains. The scientific focus, supported by the UN office of science and technology, had been aborted when Joao Frank da Costa (Brazil) took over as secretary-general in January 1977. Thereafter, substance had been shouldered aside, and those aspects of the NIEO that were of major interest to the advanced LDCs had been given priority. The result: The conference was isolated from the scientific community and the North-South scientific collaboration on fundamental issues of appropriate technology in the fields of food, energy, and health for the poorer countries was downgraded.[32] On the other hand, a rival group of UNDP advisers and Third World experts put together an alternative, development-oriented program that the United States could support, and that program ultimately played a decisive role in saving the conference from deadlock. The G-77 and the UN Secretariat were split well in advance, the conflict between Group B and the G-77 was taken for granted, and the G-77, itself, only managed to get together at the last moment.

By the time the Fifth Working Group met in May 1979, the G-77 had finally coalesced into a solid bloc, which was led by the radical Latin American group and backed by the conference secretary-general. As a result, the NIEO emphasis on technology transfer, codes of conduct, a new UN superstructure, and patent sharing took priority over the application of S&T to development. As at UNCTAD V, the draft Plan of Action prepared by the UNCSTD Secretariat "was set out almost exclusively in terms of G-77 rhetoric on the NIEO."[33] The core of the G-77 position called for the creation of three new institutional arrangements: an intergovernmental committee of the whole that would report directly to the General Assembly (bypassing ECOSOC where the DCs still had some leverage), a new S&T secretariat, and a new scientific advisory mechanism. These proposals were backed by another one for a fund to be raised by a compulsory tax on the industrialized countries, amounting to $2 billion per year by 1985 and $4 billion per year by 1990.[34]

The United States quite possibly provided more support to the Vienna conference than to any of the other UN megaconferences held during the decade of the seventies. The United States set up a working group at the ambassadorial level; engaged the interest and participation of the industrial, educational, and scientific establishments; provided masses of publicity; and fielded a high-powered sixty-five-man delegation that included four ambassadors, twenty congressional representatives, and twenty-two private-sector advisers.[35] The United States regarded UNCSTD as an opportunity to bring science to bear in a major attack on poverty; to advance equitable growth in the LDCs; to respond to the desire of the middle-income LDCs for industrialization; to mount a cooperative approach to worldwide social and economic problems; to improve the tone, quality, and content of the North-South dialogue and to minimize suspicion and distrust; and to demonstrate continued U.S. support for the UN.

However, the U.S. position was not all innocent do-goodism. The delegation's instructions included explicit reservations: no new funding, no "universal s&T information system" centered in the UN, no negotiating codes of conduct on TNCs or transfer of technology, no revision of the Paris Convention for the Protection of Industrial Property, and no new institutions.[36] Reverting again to the Kissinger style of U.S. actions at the Seventh Special Session and UNCTAD IV, the U.S. delegation carried with it a package of unilateral proposals. One proposal was for a new U.S. Institute for Scientific and Technological Cooperation (ISTC), scheduled to go into operation in 1980, which had the dual purpose of strengthening LDC s&T and focusing R&D on basic needs and global problems. Cooperative links would be established between the ISTC and institutions in other countries, DC and LDC alike. The package also included proposals for a cooperative industry program and assistance through remote sensing.[37]

The organization of the conference included a plenary session for "country statements," two committees to draw up the Program of Action, and a working group on s&T for the future — the last a group to accommodate the scientists. The Program of Action would focus on three target areas that corresponded to the three purposes of the conference, except that the second purpose was replaced by a more NIEO-oriented target, "restructuring existing patterns of international s&T relations." Committee 1 worked on Target Areas A and B, and Committee 2 worked on Target Area C, institutional and financial resources.[38]

Negotiations immediately centered on the work of Committee 2. The United States agreed to support a small two-year interim fund for s&T within the UNDP, but no new institutional development. The G-77, however, demanded a $2-billion-per-year fund that would increase to $4 billion per year by 1990. The fund would be financed by compulsory taxation on the rich nations and would be managed by a new high-level committee, open to all members of the United Nations, that would report directly to the General Assembly. The EC at first opposed both a fund and a new facility, except for the United Kingdom, which accepted the high-level committee. The OPEC countries kept well away.[39]

The conference looked like a stalemate. There was no progress the first week, and by Thursday the G-77 countries were threatening to go home if they couldn't have their way. The fate of the $50-million conference was momentarily precarious, and no one wanted to face failure. But the impasse was resolved by a weekend of work, during which the Americans, Nordics, and Japanese came around to accepting a high-level committee—but one that would report to the General Assembly through ECOSOC—a small "interim" fund, and an expert study group to look at the G-77 multi-billion-dollar scheme. The EC finally joined the other DCs, forcing the G-77 delegates to "focus on the fact that the U.S. position was the only one they would have to rally round if they wanted anything to come out of the Conference."[40]

That weekend was the turning point of the conference, at least for the crucial institutional and financial issues. After seventy-two hours of nonstop negotiations and after the EC gave in, first the East Europeans and finally, at the last moment, the G-77 agreed to a $250-million interim fund to be managed by the UNDP. A pledging conference was to be called in December, and a study group was to be established by the General Assembly.[41]

Committee 1's report on restructuring international relations (Target Area B) was never adopted. The United States had opposed the "distortion" that was built into it by the G-77, which "preferred to combine a regulatory anti-multinational corporation approach on a 'legal framework' with a recommendation for an elaborate, expensive, global information network in the UN system of doubtful usefulness or feasibility."[42] The U.S. objective had been to redirect the focus of this area, to provide practical guidance to the world community by identifying concrete and workable measures that would maximize the available technological resources for development purposes.[43] The United States and Group B therefore refused to work on codes of conduct and problems of industrial property, considering that those topics were not properly the business of UNCSTD. The working paper was passed on to the General Assembly to be transmitted eventually to the study group on S&T when it was formed. The committee did, however, force through a UN information system. Target Area A came through with the least damage, and there were forty-nine recommendations for action to strengthen the S&T capacity of the LDCs, including actions to be taken by the DCs, by international organizations, and by the LDCs themselves. The recommended actions were mainly geared toward providing institutional support, manpower, research, and information system requirements.

Finally, the conference adopted the report of the working group of scientists on s&t for the future, which provided the scientific input to the conference. This input consisted of advice from the scientific community on education, the need for governments to provide a good working environment for scientists, the need to orient science to long-term needs and technology to short- and medium-term needs, and the need for coordination between scientists and planners in government.

This last major UN conference of the decade brought several aspects of U.S. policy into clear relief. It showed that the United States remains adamantly opposed to the NIEO and anything having to do with it such as new funds or new institutions. The United States is not ungenerous and is willing to set up its own institutions for Third World assistance and to cooperate in other ways if the expense is not too great. The country would do those things in support of programs for meeting basic needs. With curious blindness, the United States seems convinced that this policy, well meaning and sometimes generous, will divert the Third World from the NIEO, despite having had U.S. offers rejected or accepted without reciprocity or modification of NIEO demands on several occasions since the Sixth Special Session. In the case of UNCSTD, the United States went to the conference to improve, among other things, the tone, quality, and content of the North-South dialogue, but it only succeeded in generating hostility and condemnation from the Third World and criticism from its own congressional delegates for reacting rather than taking the initiative. Having invested so much time, money, and interest in the conference and having maintained such a high profile, the United States was obliged to bring off a success no matter what. It did avoid a breakdown, but at the cost of compromising the U.S. position by accepting a new fund and a new organization.

The Havana Conference: The Sixth Non-Aligned Summit

It is fitting that this account of the summer of 1979 should conclude with a discussion of the Sixth Non-Aligned Summit, which met in Havana on September 3–5. The Fourth Non-Aligned Summit in Algiers in September 1973 had put together the concept of the NIEO, which led to the beginning of the North-South dialogue two years later at the Seventh Special Session. The sixth summit's Final Declaration, which includes a political and an economic declaration,[44] is something of a benchmark. It reiterates the main concepts of the NIEO as of September 1979 and summarizes the attitudes of the Non-Aligned (and, presumably, of the Third World and the G-77) toward the negotiations and the progress or lack of progress toward achieving the goals of the NIEO.

It may be asserted that the Final Declaration is a political tract that has nothing to do with development per se. But it does have everything to do with the Third World, the NIEO, and, hence, the North-South dialogue. It also reminds us that after six years of negotiation, the goals of the NIEO are unaltered and that there is more to the North-South dialogue and its conferences than economics. The declaration is also a stark retort to the illusions of the United States, exemplified at WCARRD and UNCSTD, that it can win the hearts and minds of the Third World with good intentions or even cash.

* * *

The following sections summarize the principal issues as set out in the economic section of the Final Declaration, retaining as much of the original language as possible. The sections on commodities, trade, monetary affairs, and food, which are restatements of material covered in the chapter on UNCTAD V, are not repeated. For the sake of simplicity, references to paragraphs are included in the text rather than in the notes. The acronym LDC is substituted for "the Non-Aligned and other developing countries," and "the heads of state and/or governments."

International Economic Situation. The crisis of the international economic system is a symptom of underlying structural maladjustment and basic imbalance aggravated by the unwillingness of DC market-economy countries to control their external imbalances, high levels of inflation, and unemployment resulting in the creation of new imbalances within the international economic system, and in the transfer of their adverse effects to LDCs through international trade and monetary and financial relations. This crisis also results from the persistent inequity in international economic relations characterized by dependency, exploitation, and inequality (2). The situation is unlikely to improve in the near future in view of the shortsighted and inward approach of most of the DCs to the problems besetting their internal economies and the world economy (12).

People's Struggle for Liberation. The struggle to eliminate the injustice of the existing international economic system and to establish the NIEO is an integral part of the people's struggle for political, economic, cultural, and social liberation (3) against imperialism, colonialism, neocolonialism, racism including apartheid and Zionism, and all forms of foreign domination and oppression (35).

The NIEO. The establishment of the NIEO is one of the most urgent tasks facing the Non-Aligned movement, and democratization of international economic relations constitutes its political substance (11).

The NIEO is a basic restructuring of the world economy and, in the light of past experience, the Non-Aligned reject the view that this restructuring can be achieved merely through the free play of market forces. DCs must recognize the link between structural change in their own economies and measures to generate growth in aggregate demand and productive capacity in LDCs. These structural changes include shifts in the pattern of production, consumption, and trade in the world economy; effective national control over the use of national resources; and restructuring of the international institutional framework, including the creation of new institutional arrangements, if necessary, through which LDCs would have full and effective participation in the international decision-making process (12).

Negotiating the NIEO. The NIEO has made negligible progress since the Sixth Special Session, despite numerous international conferences, owing to the lack of political will by the DCs and their dilatory, diversionary, and divisive tactics aimed at retaining their privileges in their relations with the LDCs. This is evidenced by the failure to achieve substantive results at UNCTAD V (7, 34).

LDCs deeply deplore the intransigence of most DCs and their refusal to engage in serious negotiations on the NIEO. DCs must demonstrate a real commitment to the *accepted* (italics mine) international goals, and LDCs should demonstrate their capacity to reinforce their collective bargaining power (3).

LDCs reaffirm their resolve to resist all attempts to divide and break their unity, all endeavors to seek solutions to world economic problems outside the UN framework (1). Negotiations must take place within the UN system with the General Assembly in the central role (11).

UNCTAD V. LDCs condemn the inflexible position of most DCs at UNCTAD V. They urge DCs to demonstrate their political will to resume negotiations on subjects which have been resubmitted to the TDB (35).

UNCTAD. The LDCs reaffirm recognition of UNCTAD as the principal instrument of the General Assembly for international economic negotiations on international trade and related problems of economic development (40).

The close relationship between problems and issues in the area of trade, development, money, and finance requires a global consultative mechanism within the framework of UNCTAD, which would ensure that policies of DCs are mutually consistent and supportive of the development process and also that their short-term policies promote and do not distort the restructuring of the international economy (10).

Unity. It is imperative to strengthen the unity and the joint negotiating capacity of the LDCs (7), to harmonize their diversity of interests, and to evolve a unified position on issues under negotiation (8). A key element in the struggle is ECDC on the basis of complementarity, mutual interest, solidarity, and mutual assistance in the context of the principle of self-reliance (9).

The LDCs Oppose, Reject, Condemn, or Denounce: attempts by any economic and financial institutions controlled by certain DC market-economy countries to impose measures designed to limit national sovereignty and block fundamental rights of people to develop along economic and political lines freely chosen by themselves (conditionality) (15);

all attempts to divide and break the unity of LDCs (31);

all endeavors to seek solutions to world economic problems outside the UN framework (31);

all attempts to oppose the just demands of the LDCs for restructuring the existing international economic system (31);

any attempt to make LDCs absorb the consequences of world economic crises they did not cause (32);

increasing LDC dependency as a result of increased trade or technical-scientific relations (32);

attempts to introduce concepts, norms, and principles such as "access to supplies," "graduation," "selectivity," the utilization of the so-called strategy of basic needs and the concept of differentiation to shift the focus of the international community away from negotiations on the NIEO, to distort national development priorities, or to attempt to break the unity of the LDCs (33);

all steps by some DCs to use food as a weapon (85).

OPEC. The Non-Aligned support the efforts of LDCs to seek just and remunerative prices for their exports and to improve export earnings in real terms. They condemn attempts by certain DCs to use the issue of energy to divide LDCs. The wasteful consumption pattern of DCs and the role played by transnational oil corporations have led to the squandering of hydrocarbon and depletable sources of energy. Developing country exporters had thus been subsidizing the economic growth of developed countries (23).

Persistent inflation has eroded the purchasing power of (LDC) oil exporters, prompting them to adjust oil prices in an effort to correct this situation. Transnational oil companies had been exploiting both producers and consumers and reaping windfall profits, while at the same time the imperialistic forces were falsifying facts by shifting the blame for the present situation to the developing countries exporters of oil (24).

Future Negotiations. The international energy issue should be discussed in the context of global negotiations within the United Nations with the participation of all countries and in relation to problems of development, financial and monetary reforms, world trade, and raw materials, all of which have an important bearing on the establishment of the NIEO (27).

Other Future Action of LDCs. The time has come to learn from the multiple and repeated failures of the negotiations. LDCs must have increased cohesion and willingness to struggle. It is essential to adopt new, more efficient measures, and a strong response to the dilatory tactics and maneuvers used to divide them (36). These measures include:

- promoting the integrity of the concept, objectives, and priorities of the NIEO;
- exercising full and effective permanent sovereignty and control over natural resources and other commodities and raw materials;
- exercising control over foreign capital and over the actions of TNCs;
- having the right to be considered equal parties to any international economic process (37);
- formation of producers' associations to obtain just and remunerative prices (47);
- close cooperation to facilitate concerted commodity policies (47);
- governments acceding to the Statute of the Council of Developing Country Producers and Exporters of Raw Materials Association (47);
- restricting imports from countries using protectionist devices.

TNCs and Sovereignty over Natural Resources. LDCs denounced the unacceptable policies and practices of TNCs, which, motivated by exploitative profits, exhaust the resources, distort the economies, and infringe the sovereignty of LDCs and violate the principles of nonintervention in affairs of the LDCs (70).

LDCs reaffirmed the inalienable right to exercise full, permanent sovereignty and control over their natural resources, including the right to nationalization, supervision, authority, regulation, and mutual aid to other LDCs in their struggle for political and economic independence in the face of such aggression as blockade, discrimination, boycott, pressure, and threats by imperialists, colonialists, neocolonialism, racism, including apartheid and Zionism (71).

1981 International Conference on Energy. LDCs welcome this conference and, in the meantime, recommend immediate steps in the UN system to accelerate and increase assistance to the LDCs from research in the development of new and renewable sources of energy and for ensuring access of the LDCs to the latest technology in these areas (28).

1980 Special Session on Development. It should review implementation of the NIEO, take effective measures for its establishment, and conclude the negotiations for the International Development Strategy (101).

LDCs call on DCs to reexamine their political position on most international economic problems so as to enable the special session to adopt effective guidelines to action.

The world economic crisis, the difficult economic situation faced by LDCs, and the limited advance in negotiations for the NIEO justify that the special session should be held at a political level appropriate to the gravity of these problems (104).

* * *

Comment

The Sixth Non-Aligned Summit should be seen as another episode in the continuing Third World struggle to maintain unity. At the time, the greatest threat was the battle for leadership between Tito and Fidel Castro, or between the "non-aligned" Non-Aligned and those countries that would "tilt" toward the Soviet Union, which Castro tried to promote as the champion of the Third World.[45] He had much to gain if he played his cards right, and he pushed as hard as he could without provoking an outright breach in the ranks. A second threat was the split over oil between OPEC and non-OPEC LDCs, which had surfaced so ominously at UNCTAD V. These threats were avoided, however, by shifting the focus of the summit toward the North-South perspective, so that the United States became the principal target for grievances, something upon which all could happily unite. The OPEC countries were then portrayed as fellow victims of the imperialist exploiters, more to be pitied than censured. The "tilt" toward the Soviets was finessed by a denunciation of "hegemony." The Final Declaration, therefore, became a concerted attack on the United States, demanding an end to that country's intransigent opposition to the NIEO and to the evil system the United States supported.

How seriously should one take the Final Declaration? As a document it has many faults. It is a cut-and-paste job, and not a very good one at that. It is badly organized; repetitive; festooned with political jargon, clichés, and platitudes; simplistic; and grandiose. It reads less like a serious document on international relations than a religious tract sorting out the world in two camps, the good and the evil. Nevertheless, it is a serious document that should not be dismissed out of hand. It is a reassertion of Third World unity, an unimpaired endorsement of the NIEO after six years of failure, and a vigorous statement of intent.

Above all, it presents the NIEO more clearly than ever as a political program. The declaration declares unmitigated hostility toward the present order and those countries that support it. It presents the NIEO, not as a compromise, but as a nonnegotiable replacement for the present international economic system. It sees the world in exclusively Third World or "bloc" terms. Toward unity and the achievement of its ends, the Third World is prepared to subordinate everything, to sacrifice the goodwill of donor nations, and to reject assistance for basic needs, foreign investment, and cooperation in technology. The declaration shows that the Third World is willing to make sacrifices and to suffer the ruinous escalation of oil prices in order to maintain its unity and its ideological position. The document calls for a political-level meeting at the Special Session on Development. Evidence of this politicization was demonstrated at UNIDO III in early 1980 (see Chapter 6), in spite of the fact that the conference broke up as a result. With these words and actions, the Third World appears to be carrying out the decision made by the meeting of wise men at Arusha in December 1978 to move from petition to pressure and action.

Summary

The summer of 1979 ended on a shrill and discordant note. The soothing platitudes that followed UNCTAD V about a continuing dialogue, an honest outcome, and a marketplace of ideas — designed to put a good face on things — were blown away by the gusty denunciations of the Havana Summit. Not that the summer had been all that placid. OPEC, goaded into action by UNCTAD V, had thrown down the gauntlet to the West at OPEC's own summit in June, calling for a new round of negotiations on a broad front and jacking up the price of oil another 20 percent for good measure. Although the United States tried to convince itself it had gotten off easy at UNCTAD V, the G-77 demonstrated in Rome and again in Vienna that it had not given an inch on the NIEO and all but turned both WCARRD and UNCSTD into mini-UNCTAD vs. Those were summer storms. Havana generated a hurricane, blasting Western intransigence in general and the United States in particular in a no-holds-barred denunciation.

To paraphrase Mark Twain, the post–UNCTAD V reports of the death of the North-South dialogue were greatly exaggerated. That UNCTAD V was a low point for the dialogue cannot be denied. The doldrums since CIEC, of which I have sketched the latest chapter, generated much pessimism and discouragement. Nevertheless, the North-South dialogue would not, indeed could not, go away. Remaining from UNCTAD V was the unfinished business of negotiating the Common Fund articles of agreement, the codes of conduct for TNCs and for the transfer of technology, the conference on RBPS, and a multitude of other items referred back to the TDB. Intense preparations were already under way on the International Development Strategy for the Third Development Decade, for the UNGA Special Session on Development, and for the comprehensive global negotiations that were likely to go on for months like the CIEC. "We have come full-circle, it seems," said U.S. negotiator Meissner, wearily, "back to the CIEC formula all over again."[46]

Rude Awakening

With the Havana Final Declaration still ringing in Washington's ears, the G-77, which had already met in a ministerial session, formally presented the idea of global negotiations to the UN Committee of the Whole (cow), which then "commended" the idea to the General Assembly at its Thirty-fourth Session.[1] The General Assembly then passed enabling resolutions (34/138 and 34/139)[2] that provided for holding the Eleventh Special Session of the General Assembly in 1980 to launch a round of "global and sustained negotiations," "action oriented and proceeding in a simultaneous manner," in order to ensure a coherent and integrated approach to the issues under negotiation. Negotiations would take place within the UN system and include issues in the fields of raw materials, energy, trade, development, money, and finance.

Thus, three activities would be addressed at the Eleventh Special Session: (1) evaluation of the nieo, (2) adoption of a new International Development Strategy (ids) for the eighties, and (3) the launching of global negotiations on international economic cooperation and development. Evaluation of the nieo was assigned to the office of the secretary-general (33/198). The International Development Strategy for the Third UN Development Decade (dd iii) was assigned to a special preparatory committee (33/193). Preparation of the global negotiations was assigned to the cow (34/138). These actions set the basic pattern for further work on development and the nieo within the UN framework for the rest of 1979 and 1980.

Secretary Vance set the tone and framework for U.S. policy in his speech to the General Assembly on September 24.[3] He was, as might as have been expected, cautious, conservative, and responsible. Taking the traditional Vance overview, he spoke of a world of complexity and rapid change, of a "profusion of different systems and allegiances and a diffusion of political and military power," and of an end to the "unrelenting hostility of the Cold War." But, he warned, "despite our emergence from the days of unrelenting hostility, the East-West relationship can deteriorate dangerously whenever one side fails to respect the security interests of the other." It was a prescient utterance.

Referring to the challenges of the eighties, Vance mentioned some of the gains already made—increases in IMF resources, an increased lending capacity, expanded trade opportunities, and progress on debt and the Common Fund. But, he stressed, the problems ahead would be not only difficult but profound. They were too important, he said, to lapse again into confrontation and "unleash a spiral of rhetoric" or resort to economic nationalism and protection. Another prescient utterance.

The central question, he said, was energy, which, in a "future of greater scarcity," threatened to divide countries economically and politically. The United States was not only dedicated to solving its own energy problem but to helping others with theirs. He announced that in October the United States would establish the Institute for Scientific and Technological Cooperation that had been announced at UNCSTD in August.

The third common problem, after peace and energy, was basic economic and social rights. Toward this end, he said, "We must each strive to move the North-South dialogue beyond grand themes and on to specific cases, to priority areas in which practical development goals can be met"—to food security, population control, and refugee and disaster relief.

Finally, with regard to global negotiations, Vance said that the United States would participate in the COW in consultations to decide the most effective way of conducting such negotiations. He urged participants to be realistic about each other's political and economic capabilities, to assign priorities to issues on which concrete results could be achieved, and to avoid duplicating the work of existing institutions.

There were no surprises in Vance's speech nor even any variations from the standard lines of U.S. policy.

Afghanistan

But there were surprises; they came from Southwest Asia. The United States was trying to digest the capture of its Tehran embassy staff when a mob of youths burned the embassy in Islamabad on November 21, and the staff barely escaped with their lives. Then, on December 27, the Soviet Union invaded Afghanistan. During the previous three days the Soviet Union had airlifted 5,000 troops into Kabul, and five more Soviet divisions had been moved up to the Afghan frontier. Thursday night, December 27, Afghanistan's president since September, Hafizullah Amin, was killed (executed or assassinated), and a new president, Soviet protégé Babrak Karmal, was installed in his place. By December 30, there were 25,000 Soviet troops in Afghanistan, and by January 4, 1980, 50,000 were dispersing toward the Afghan borders with Pakistan and Iran. It was a stunning coup de main and the first time since World War II (outside of Eastern Europe) that Soviet combat troops had played an overt role in support of a Soviet Union political intervention outside its borders.

The world was shocked, not only by the Soviet demonstration of naked power but by its suddenness. Why? What did it mean? What were the Soviets' intentions? Where would it stop? Such an intervention in a volatile area next to the Persian Gulf spelled high danger, certainly a revival of East-West hostility, and possibly war. Only two events in post–World War II history — the Suez crisis of October 1956 and the Cuban missile crisis of October 1962 — come close to the invasion of Afghanistan in shock value.

World leaders, North and South alike, who were not a part of the Soviet sphere condemned the invasion. President Carter, in a special address to the nation on January 4, warned that the invasion was "an extremely serious threat to peace . . . a callous violation of international law and the UN Charter."[4] The Italian Communist party called the invasion a violation of the principle of independence. India held back, cautioning against acts that might aggravate the situation. NATO "senior members" met on Monday December 31 in London to assess the situation and to explore possible common actions. On January 14, the General Assembly in special session passed a resolution — not mentioning the Soviet Union by name — deploring the recent armed intervention, which was inconsistent with the principles of the UN Charter concerning respect for sovereignty, territorial integrity, and political independence, and calling for an immediate withdrawal of foreign troops (A/RES/E5-6/2). Out of 152 member-nations, 104 (including 60 of the 96 Non-Aligned nations) voted for the resolution; 18, against it (Warsaw Pact and client-states, e.g., Vietnam and Cuba); 18 abstained; and 12 were absent.[5]

The impact of the invasion on the United States was profound and accelerated its increasing preoccupation with defense. During 1979, the administration had gone to great lengths to avoid any act that might dampen the spirit of détente and endanger the SALT II Treaty signed in Vienna on June 18, 1979. At the same time, the administration had had to face domestic criticism from congressional conservatives in both parties that SALT II was a "sellout," that the United States was negotiating from weakness, not strength, and that Senate approval would be contingent on improving the U.S. defense capability. By December, Carter had been stating publicly that defense spending would be increased by 5 percent to keep up with the Soviets, and in reference to the creation of the rapid deployment force (RDF) concept, he had said, "We must understand that not every instance of the firm application of power is a potential Vietnam."[6] That last statement was another step away from the hands-off policy of the seventies. Afghanistan cleared the air, put an end to caution, and unified the United States behind a strong policy of defense and deterrence.

This sudden catalyzing of the national spirit was given formal and comprehensive articulation by the president in his January 23, 1980, State of the Union Address and Message to the Congress.[7] He had worked long and studiously on his speech, studying old government reports and history texts to see how his predecessors had handled international crises. There was a sense of personal crisis, for Carter had come into the White House as a man of peace, had been determined to lower tensions between the United States and the Soviet Union, had believed he was making progress, and now felt "betrayed" by Brezhnev over Afghanistan.[8] The result was a major foreign policy restatement, the most important of Carter's administration.

Continuing the theme of his February 1979 speech at Georgia Tech, Carter said that the decade of the eighties had been born in turmoil, strife, and change and was "a time of challenge to our interests and values." The focus of attention was on the Middle East, but the problems were worldwide. Peace and freedom depended on the United States and on its steadfastness of purpose in a "world wracked by change and turmoil." "The nation," he said, "is no longer tempted by isolationism." In a statement reminiscent of President Kennedy, Carter said, "America must pay whatever price is required to remain the strongest nation in the world to deter adversaries and support friends and allies." The United States must also support global economic growth through expanded trade and development assistance. The United States, he said, has a common interest with the vast majority of the world's nations, who are striving to preserve their independence, and with peoples who are aspiring to political freedom and economic development. The United States would "continue to build ties with developing nations, helping to strengthen their national independence" and their ability to resist outside agression. "We are striving to build a world," he said, "in which peoples with diverse interests can live freely and prosper."

Carter stressed the continuity of U.S. policy, the steadfastness of purpose of a nation "no longer tempted by isolationism," continued support for the evolution of the free nations throughout the Third World, and continued support for global economic growth. He was right to do so. For, in what has since become known as the Carter Doctrine, he restated, in his own terms, the basic foreign policy doctrine of the United States since its original articulation by President Truman in 1947. The statement marked the end of the Nixon Doctrine, of the decade of withdrawal, and the resumption of the traditional U.S. role in the world. As one official put it, the speech was "a sustained and steady commitment to the long pull, not a dramatic bugle-led charge for a short-lived tactical victory."[9]

The response from Congress and the American people was overwhelmingly favorable, and Carter's sagging popularity shot up in the polls. For the moment, at least, the question of Carter's lack of leadership faded, and Congress began to move with speed on some major items of administration legislation. House Speaker Thomas O'Neill promised favorable House action on Carter's lagging energy program announced in July after the Tokyo Summit: the $227-billion windfall profits tax, the creation of an energy mobilization board and an energy security corporation. National patriotism — all but buried during the late sixties, moribund during the seventies, and stung by the Iranian students taking U.S. embassy personnel hostage — surged in a mixture of America-first, anti-Khomeini, anti-Soviet fervor.

The Soviet invasion of Afghanistan broke the spell of the seventies for Americans, and it shattered the illusion of detachment and isolation into which the country had retreated. Suddenly, the United States was again totally involved, and the threat to its security was, not an unbelievable religious mystic or incomprehensible figures of oil imports and payments deficits, but the clear-cut, eminently recognizable image of the Russian bear slouching toward the Persian Gulf. That was something any American could understand. It was a rude awakening, and there could be no going back to sleep.

The impact on U.S. priorities was powerful as secondary effects rippled through the world system. The invasion marked the reopening of the Cold War and a return to bipolarity, which most authorities, including Henry Kissinger and Cyrus Vance as recently as the latter's speech to the Thirty-fourth General Assembly, had declared to be at an end. It brought a sharp shock to the Western alliance. Disagreement over the appropriate responses to Afghanistan and the hostage crisis produced, on the one hand, the most serious rift in the alliance since the Suez crisis and, on the other, a Soviet "peace offensive" to exploit it. Third World relations were suddenly set in relief.

There had already been an increasing awareness by the U.S. administration of the importance of the Third World as a trading partner, since U.S. exports to the Third World during the seventies had exceeded U.S. exports to Europe and Japan combined. The Afghanistan invasion also renewed the United States' awareness of the importance of the Third World in the balance of power between the superpowers. Whether the Third World liked it or not, overt competition between East and West would occur and was occurring in Southeast Asia, South Asia, the Middle East, Africa, and Central America. Some Third World leaders were even beginning to question the realism of nonalignment. But how directly these events and perceptions would affect U.S. policy toward the NIEO remained to be seen. The test case would be the Eleventh Special Session in August 1980.

UNIDO III

The North-South establishment received another rude shock during late January and February 1980, this time from the South at the Third Conference of the United Nations Industrial Development Organization (UNIDO) held in New Delhi from January 21 through February 9, 1980.[10] UNIDO had become a primary vehicle for promoting the NIEO when UNIDO II, held in Lima, Peru, in 1975, adopted the Lima Declaration and Plan of Action, which set forth goals for the industrialization of developing countries as an integral component of the establishment of the NIEO and specified the means by which the international community as a whole might take supportive action. It will be recalled that UNIDO II was held after the Sixth Special Session and the Twenty-ninth General Assembly, when the United States was still locked in a posture of confrontation. The United States was the only country at Lima to vote against the resolution as a whole. The New Delhi conference met (1) to review progress toward implementation of the Lima Declaration, (2) to make an appraisal of the major policies, problems, and obstacles involved, and (3) to produce a strategy for further industrialization as an essential element of the development process of the 1980s and beyond.[11] The most controversial proposal of the UNIDO Secretariat, "Industry 2000" (ID/Conf.4/3), called for UNIDO III to create a new multilateral financial mechanism to promote industrialization.

What made the conference particularly controversial lay in the G-77 negotiating paper, the Havana Declaration, adopted at a ministerial meeting of the G-77 in Havana in December 1979. The Havana Declaration (tabled as ID/Conf.4/CRP.13) was essentially the G-77 counterpart to the Havana Final Declaration of the Non-Aligned. It reiterated the economic doctrines of the NIEO, CERDS, and the Lima Declaration; included the extreme ideological statements of the Final Declaration; and proposed the establishment of a $300-billion fund.

The Group B negotiating paper,[12] drafted by the OECD Secretariat, restated the basic Group B positions concerning maintenance of the open international economic system; opposition to "targets"; emphasis on gradual economic evolution, appropriate industrialization, and technology; the supplementary role of ODA; and the importance of private investment.

Those positions have already been reviewed at length elsewhere and need not be repeated here. It is sufficient to present the focus of the differences, which was the G-77 demand for the establishment of a $300-billion fund.

The bulk of the resources were to come from the DCs plus countries with "excess liquidity," the fund was to be administered by the LDCs, and financing was to be provided on soft terms. The U.S. and Group B position, stated in the U.S. delegation's "Scope Paper"[13] and reiterated in the "U.S. Statement" by Ambassador John W. McDonald Jr., was to oppose new financial mechanisms or massive transfer proposals and to focus the work of the conference on improving the effectiveness of UNIDO as a technical assistance organization. The U.S. negotiators were expecting trouble, even a blowup, because of the conflicting objectives.

Limitations of space do not permit a review of the item-by-item negotiations, except to state that the opposing positions on technology, energy, finance, transnational corporations, investment, and redeployment were essentially the same opposing positions that had been taken at earlier conferences. In the event, the formal negotiations at UNIDO III hardly mattered.

After discussing mainly procedural questions in Committees 1 and 2,[14] the G-77 proposed to substitute the New Delhi Plan of Action (ID/Conf.4/CRP.16 Add.1) in Committee 1 and the New Delhi Declaration (ID Conf.4/CRP.16) and the Plan of Action in Committee 2 for the agenda as a basis for discussion. Group B demanded that the committees stick to the agenda that had been agreed upon. In Committee 1, the chairman (Zaire) accepted the Group B demand, but on the third day, the G-77 moved to set aside the agenda in order to introduce the New Delhi Plan of Action as the basis for discussion. This action was permitted on the understanding that the committee would then return to the agenda. The practical effect, however, was to permit the G-77 to draw on the New Delhi Plan of Action in addressing agenda items, including the establishment of the $300-billion fund. Committee 2 also compromised by agreeing to follow the agenda but to use the Plan of Action as the substantive base of the discussion.[15]

Thus, the New Delhi Declaration and Plan of Action became the focus for the deliberations and the basic text of the proposed conference report. It was a skillful G-77 tactic to dominate the substance of the conference, essentially the same tactic that had been used to such effect at the Sixth Special Session of the General Assembly. It gave the G-77 the initiative and left Group B to react.

The two working groups formed from the committees to draft the final conference report became bogged down by the end of the second week because of the sheer volume of work—seventy pages of text. The United States proposed establishing a third working group to concentrate on the Declaration and leaving the Plan of Action to the other two working groups. Group B then submitted a revised text of the conference report (10/Conf.4/CRP.18) on February 5. However, 95 percent of it was deleted by the G-77, including language derived from UNCTAD V, UNGA resolutions, and even the Lima Declaration — the G-77 arguing that those were in the past and that the conference should look to the future. "The stage was set for a major confrontation."[16]

In a last-ditch effort to avoid that confrontation, Group B and G-77 leaders agreed to create a president's contact group. The chairman, Indian Secretary of Industry S. S. Marathe (acting in place of the conference's president, P. V. Narasinha Rao), produced a new president's "compromise" text of both the Declaration and the Plan of Action. The contact group met round the clock for the next two days, and the conference was extended for a day. Group B finally decided to abstain on the document as a whole and asked for a paragraph-by-paragraph vote so it could vote against some twenty paragraphs of the text. It also informed the president that if he then withdrew his compromise text and the G-77 resubmitted the original text, Group B would vote against the entire document, both the Declaration and the Plan of Action. In the event, the president did withdraw his text, and the G-77 pushed its version through, passing it by a vote of 83 for and 22 against.[17]

The U.S. representative reported that there were many, many things wrong with the G-77 text. It was heavily laden with harsh political language that was totally unacceptable to the West. In economic terms, "[it] blamed the West for all the world's ills and made the G-77 (including OPEC) the good guys. It also reactivated the highly contentious language of [CERDS] and tried to make UNIDO into a global financial institution rivaling the IBRD/IMF and gave it more power over trade issues than UNCTAD and the GATT combined."[18]

Not surprisingly, each side blamed the other for the failure of UNIDO III.[19] Marathe blamed Group B for "offering no important compromise to which the G-77 moderates could rally." UNIDO Executive Director Abd-El Rahman Khane declared that the legitimate and urgent needs of the Third World could not be delayed. Conference President Rao stated that the onus for disagreement lay "squarely in one quarter." The U.S. representative reported that a few hours before the close of the conference, Mexico's delegate had told him that he was pleased with the confrontation "they had achieved," because the G-77 wanted to use this failure as a means of pressuring the West to be more forthcoming during future global negotiations, that a blowup had to come sooner or later, and that he was glad to get it out of the way and cared little for its impact on UNIDO. It was generally believed that the breakdown was deliberately engineered by the G-77 radicals, that they had forced the G-77 text through knowing that the language was so extreme that no agreement was possible.

In conclusion, UNIDO III is another name to add to the list of failed enterprises. The manner of its passing is incidental; what it eloquently demonstrated was that the protagonists were not yet willing or able to rise above diplomatic-level perspectives. That the G-77 radicals deliberately engineered a confrontation is likely. That the United States expected a confrontation but would or could do nothing to avert it was a contribution by default. That the confrontation came on the eve of the publication of the report of the Brandt Commission, *North-South: A Programme for Survival,*[20] was ironic.

Unfinished Business

On a lower level, the months following the Thirty-fourth General Assembly were busy and not wholly barren. Headline conferences such as UNCTAD V and UNIDO III overshadow the multitude of lesser negotiations and consultations on North-South issues. As of May 1980, the Department of State was engaged in negotiations on thirteen active commodity items in addition to the Common Fund, on eleven items of business in the trade sector, on three in transportation, five in business and investment, twelve in ODA, eleven in other financial and monetary issues, six in technology, eight in food, seven in new and renewable sources of energy, and eleven miscellaneous items for a total of eighty-eight — all within the parameters of the North-South dialogue.[21] Among the negotiations were the important ongoing revision of the Paris Convention, the UN Conference on Restrictive Business Practices, and conferences on the Common Fund articles and the code of conduct on the transfer of technology.

The Paris Convention

The Diplomatic Conference to Revise the Paris Convention for the Protection of Industrial Property was held in Geneva under the auspices of WIPO. Its first session ended on March 4, 1980, but it had consisted of only a preliminary discussion of a few noncontroversial substantive issues. A two-thirds voting majority to adopt the final revised text of the convention was accepted over U.S. objections. The conference decided to reconvene in Nairobi in the spring of 1981.[22]

UN Conference on Restrictive Business Practices

On April 27, 1980, the UN Conference on Restrictive Business Practices called for by UNCTAD V adopted a set of Rules of Restrictive Business Practices, bringing to a successful close efforts that had begun in Nairobi in 1976.[23] The rules extend the concept of home country responsibility for the regulation of practices of enterprises from domestic practices only to prac-

tices carried out within the economies of other countries. Restrictive practices are defined as acts that limit access to markets or otherwise restrain
competition, having adverse effects on international trade and development, particularly of LDCs.

The rules met U.S. concerns by applying to both governments and
business, by being voluntary rather than mandatory, and by incorporating
U.S. and other Western antitrust philosophies. The rules were to be
adopted by the General Assembly at its Thirty-fifth session.[24] Institutional
machinery is to be provided by an international group of experts operating
within the framework of a committee of UNCTAD. UNCTAD acclaimed the
agreement as a "major step forward on the road to implementing the New
International Economic Order" and observed wistfully, "Last but not least,
the agreement represents a success of multilateral diplomacy,
demonstrating that there exists a capacity for governments to negotiate
within the framework of UNCTAD not only, as is often alleged, resolutions,
but also complex instruments of a wide-ranging character.[25]

The Common Fund

At midnight on June 27, 1980, after five sessions of an interim committee that had been formed to draft the precise articles of agreement, the UN
Negotiating Conference on the Common Fund adopted Articles of Agreement in its fourth session.[26] UNCTAD Secretary-General Corea was
understandably pleased and called the agreement a major breakthrough.
He said it provided "powerful proof of the capacity of the entire international community acting through the UN to negotiate concrete and complex matters."[27] But, he cautioned, that agreement was only the first step,
and efforts should be made to achieve universal membership and to en-
courage the conclusion of new commodity agreements.

For the United States, the articles were an improved version of the
"framework agreement." The United States will have a seat on both the
governing council and the executive board. Important financial and constitutional decisions will require a 75 percent vote, which means the United
States and Group B will have blocking power if they need it since they have
a combined voting strength of 42 percent. OPEC will pay the $1-million fee
of the LLDCs plus its own share. The United States will contribute to the first
window but has no obligation (or intention) to pay into the second.

The U.S. Congress will still have to approve the agreement as a treaty
unless it is completed as an executive agreement. Even then, Congress will
have to approve the $70-million U.S. contribution. To do so, Congress will
have to be assured that the Common Fund will have something to do. So
far the cocoa talks have collapsed, and coffee is not expected to produce buf-

fer stocks since the practical operation of nationally controlled buffer stocks would be difficult. Only rubber and tin have commodity agreements and would be eligible for participation in the Common Fund.[28]

Code of Conduct on the Transfer of Technology

The UN Conference on an International Code of Conduct on the Transfer of Technology, which adjourned on March 9, 1979, reconvened for a second session in October. For three weeks it concentrated on a compromise text on all substantive issues except the legal nature of the code and the nature of the institutional machinery, the two main sticking points at the first session and at UNCTAD V.[29] The second session adjourned on November 16, and it had made some progress. A resumed session in April 1980 failed to reach agreement on restrictive practices and applicable law, and another session was not expected before 1981.[30]

Thus, the record of these months of lower-level negotiations since the Thirty-fourth General Assembly elicits both congratulation and condemnation, as appropriate, but in a curiously muted fashion. Attention was already moving away from interest in the "leftovers" from Phase 1 of the dialogue to the newer concerns of recycling, debt, adjustment, massive transfers, and ECDC, the spectrum of largely energy-related issues that had begun to take shape at Arusha, gathered force at Havana, and surfaced boldly at UNIDO III. Significant events and activities during that period included the IMF annual meeting at Belgrade in September 1979; the signing of Lomé II (the EC-ACP aid agreement in October 1979); continuing work in the preparatory committee on the IDS for DD III; and negotiations within G-77 and Non-Aligned circles for a common policy on energy, particularly the recommendations of the joint G-77/Non-Aligned meeting in Georgetown, Guyana, in August 1979. But all thinking and planning was increasingly focused on the global negotiations and the Eleventh Special Session of the General Assembly that was scheduled for late August 1980.

Toward Global Negotiations

Preparations for the Eleventh Special Session began in the Committee of the Whole (COW), which had been created by the Thirty-second General Assembly in the autumn of 1977 as a follow-up forum to CIEC. The United States took a genuine interest in creating the COW, which it envisaged as a high-level (ministerial) body in which leaders could meet to get down to basics or carry on a continuing dialogue to communicate, learn, and educate. But a truly successful COW was not to be. The G-77 saw the committee as an operational-level instrument that would keep up the pressure for the NIEO. On the eve of the Thirty-third General Assembly in 1978, a consensus or "agreed conclusions" on the role of the COW foundered over the question of whether or not the COW would be a forum for negotiation or one for consultation only.[31] The COW became a disappointment to both North and South, and the United States quickly lost its original high interest. Undersecretary of State for Economic Affairs Richard N. Cooper attended one session, stayed until three in the morning, and never returned.

Nevertheless, the General Assembly turned to the COW for action on the special session. Beginning in late 1979, in accordance with Resolution 34/138, the COW devoted itself entirely to preparations for the global negotiations, and its goal was a finished product for action at the Eleventh Special Session. Not surprisingly, the committee's efforts yielded little agreement as North and South produced contrasting proposals and views.

The U.S. objective had been for the global negotiations to focus on a narrow, relatively simple range of issues, e.g., alternative energy resources, food security, protectionism, financial flows, and health; to increase Third World willingness to negotiate constructively on the environment, radio frequencies, the Law of the Sea,[32] and other "global issues" to give the United States a positive image; and to recycle OPEC surpluses to deficit LDCs. The United States and Group B countries also wanted the global negotiations to be decentralized — that is, to have the work load distributed throughout the international system — and they wanted the negotiations to provide guidance rather than result in mandatory rules.[33]

The G-77 wanted the negotiations to be comprehensive, based on the NIEO, and centered at the United Nations in New York rather than dispersed. They wanted to address simultaneously the five subject areas of commodities, trade, energy, development, and money and finance, and they wanted binding results.[34]

Through the first half of 1980 the COW remained stalemated on all points, and the negotiations were desultory and uninspired. The committee concluded its final substantive session on July 4, 1980, having failed to agree on proposals for the agenda, procedures, or timeframe of the global negotiations.[35] Nevertheless, the COW adopted a draft agenda for the Eleventh Special Session, which included approval of the new International Development Strategy for Third World development, a report on progress toward the NIEO, and consideration of global negotiations.[36]

In a closing statement, Chairman Bogdan Crobrnja (Yugloslavia) said that one of the main features of the committee's work had been the rigidity of the various viewpoints. The G-77, he said, had been a little late to show flexibility, but he was not convinced that if they had done so earlier it would have done any good because of the rigidity of the industrialized countries.[37]

Congressional Lag

The U.S. efforts were faring no better in Washington where Congress was making empty rhetoric out of the administration's commitments to increased international economic assistance and cooperation. In September 1979, the House of Representatives, in passing a $7.75-billion foreign aid appropriation for fiscal year 1980, forbade the use of U.S. funds for "indirect aid" to Vietnam, Cambodia, Laos, the Central African Empire, Angola, or Cuba. By effectively stopping U.S. contributions to the World Bank, and putting an end to the operations of the Bank's soft-loan affiliate, the International Development Association (IDA), the House cut off assistance to the poorest, most needy, and most dependent nations of the Third World. In January 1980, the House refused to ratify the agreement doubling the World Bank's capital — a $40-billion increase approved by the IBRD governors, which was necessary to keep up the levels of lending through 1985. In March, a House-Senate conference committee finally agreed on an $8.1-billion aid budget for fiscal year 1980 ($680 million less than had been requested), but the agreement was aborted when Congress suddenly discovered that the FY 1980 budget had broken through the spending ceiling. The failure of the agreement meant that U.S. aid reverted to the 1979 level.

The change also meant abandoning all new spending measures. Thus, the U.S. contributions to new replenishments of regional development banks were kept pending, as was the rendering of overdue final installments on old replenishments. By May, Food for Peace funds had been exhausted. A bill to permit the United States to participate in the 50 percent quota increase of the IMF met strong opposition in the House, where some people opposed it on the grounds that it represented a back-door rescue of the commercial banks that had "overloaned" to Third World countries.

The reasons for the general breakdown are complex, but they include a continuation of a traditional dislike of aid, inordinate delays in reaching agreement in conference between the House and the Senate, and further delays owing to a fear of bringing the conference report to the floor of Congress after the events in Afghanistan and Iran.[38]

The breakdown was not due to a lack of administration support. Secretary Vance, in his FY 1981 economic assistance presentation to the Congress, stressed the increasing importance of the Third World to U.S. interests, including increased competition from the Soviet Union.[39] Assistant Secretary of the Treasury for International Affairs C. Fred Bergsten, in a May 15 statement before the subcommittees on International Economic Policy and Trade and on International Organization of the House Foreign Affairs Committee, declared that congressional action was urgent on several pieces of commodity legislation, on the latest IMF quota increase, on authority and appropriations legislation for MDBS, the IBRD general capital increase, and the IDA sixth replenishment. Failure to act, he said, weakens U.S. influence in those institutions (the U.S. vote in the IMF would drop from 21 percent to 15 percent) and "in overall North-South relations and leads other donor countries to doubt our pledges across a wide range of negotiations"; it also "damages the moral, political and economic leadership role of the U.S."[40]

On May 28, Deputy Secretary of State Warren Christopher told the Council on Foreign Relations that the United States has "little chance to be positive when we face the world with empty pockets." He stressed that "We must lay to rest the illusion that foreign policy successes can be underwritten on the cheap."[41]

On July 2, Secretary Edmund Muskie spoke out for the second time against Congress's failure to act.[42] In a speech to the Foreign Policy Association, he blamed the delays on a lack of political will rather than on parliamentary difficulties. He pointed out that not only did people suffer as a result, but so did U.S. influence, diplomacy, and credibility. He expressed concern at a developing pattern of failure to back rhetoric about leadership with "the costs of leadership." He feared the consequences of isolation, a declining U.S. influence, and—reiterating former Secretary Vance's theme—an inability of the United States to compete in the Third World with the Soviets.[43]

This failure to pay "the costs of leadership" in the Third World stands in contrast to the President Carter's request for a 3 percent increase in defense spending and congressional action that increased that request to 5 percent, the largest single increase in defense spending in post–World War II history. Congress's actions set in relief the relative weights given—at least during 1980—to the two foreign policy priorities, defense and Third World relations.

Development assistance is not by any means the whole of the United States' economic relations with the Third World, and compared to the total value of trade, investment, security assistance, economic relations, and social relations, it is trifling. But development assistance stands at the center of political relations—as was reflected in the NIEO, the Havana Final Declaration of the Non-Aligned, and the Havana Declaration of the G-77—and of the United States credibility in the United Nations. The assistance is substantially more important than the sums involved would suggest.

The Venice Summit

So far in this chapter, I have followed two main themes through the months after the Thirty-fourth General Assembly — the continuing North-South dialogue and the sudden crisis in East-West relations and within the Atlantic alliance brought about by the Soviet invasion of Afghanistan. Those two themes, which appear to be largely independent in terms of policy and action, were brought together at the economic summit of the seven leading Western industrial nations held in Venice in June 1980.

On the official agenda were the economic issues of recession, inflation, energy, oil prices, recycling, and development. The unofficial agenda included the disarray into which Western relations had been thrown by Afghanistan and Iran, the friction over the U.S. sanctions policy, the Olympic boycott, détente, and, overall, the question of U.S. leadership. The Soviet Union, with tiresome persistence, chose the eve of the meeting to announce the withdrawal of some of the 85,000 troops then in Afghanistan. That immediately became another item on the unofficial agenda and what one State Department official called "a great public relations stunt."[44] The United States was also very much concerned that West German Chancellor Schmidt might accept a freeze on new medium-range nuclear missiles at his meeting with President Brezhnev scheduled for the week following the Venice meeting. There would, inevitably, be another Carter plea for economic sanctions on grain and high technology and for joint action on Iran. It was a tall order for a two-day meeting.

Nevertheless, the Venice Summit seems to have been successful; in many ways, it was as if the bell had rung and it was time to sit down and behave. The group responded to the Soviet "gesture" on Afghanistan with the crisp statement that "in order to make a useful contribution, this withdrawal, if confirmed, will have to be permanent and continue until the complete withdrawal of the Soviet troops."[45] Chancellor Schmidt's position on theater nuclear weapons was "clarified" during a ninety-minute private meeting in Carter's hotel room, after which the president told reporters that he had "absolutely no doubt" that the West German chancellor would carry out their agreement on the missiles.[46] President Carter agreed to modify his hard line on the Soviet Union; instead of demanding the withdrawal of Soviet troops from Afghanistan, he would accept the possibility of negotiation. But, he cautioned, Europe could not be an island of détente while aggression was carried out elsewhere. A joint statement was issued that condemned the holding of the hostages in Iran. No statements were issued, however, on the key question of sanctions toward either the Soviet Union or Iran.

The official business of the summit was reported in the Summit Declaration.[47] Like the previous Tokyo Summit, emphasis had been placed on energy, the rising price of oil "bearing no relation to market conditions," the consequent inflation, financial distortion, economic slowdown, trade deficits, and the enormous hardships for the non-OPEC developing countries. The common recommendations adopted were for recycling OPEC surpluses to the Third World and for all countries, not only the industrialized world, to break the existing link between economic growth and consumption of oil.

"Relations with Developing Countries" (Section 4) had been a major subject. In their concluding statements, all leaders had emphasized the importance of finding effective solutions to the problems of the developing countries. Both Schmidt and Canadian Premier Trudeau had endorsed the Brandt Commission's recommendation for a North-South summit. The declaration expressed concern over the impact of oil prices on LDCs. It looked forward to the global negotiations with "a positive spirit," especially for cooperation on energy conservation and development, the expansion of exports, an enhancement of human skills, and the tackling of the underlying food and population problems.

The summit nations asked the World Bank to examine the adequacy of the available resources for developing conventional and renewable energy resources in oil-importing developing countries. The declaration stated that the seven nations were ready to join the developing countries in "comprehensive long-term strategies" to increase food production and to improve grain storage and food handling facilities. The report urged that a high priority be given to efforts to cope with population growth, and it supported the general capital increase of the World Bank, the sixth replenishment of the IDA, and increases in the funding of the regional development banks (RDBs). The declaration also stated that the democratic, industrialized countries could not carry the sole responsibility for aid to developing countries, it must be shared by the oil-exporting countries and the industrialized Communist countries. What stood out among the many familiar proposals was the emphasis that was given to the Third World at a time of high East-West tension and grave economic problems.

President Carter seemed to have evolved from something of an outsider tolerated by the European "professionals" to a first among equals. This time he had had a clear objective and, with it, a force and consistency hitherto lacking. The news that the United States had made more progress on energy conservation than any of the other participants deepened the impact of his words. At last he seemed to move among his peers with confidence and understanding. This time he did not return to Washington a troubled man seeking retreat at Camp David. He was exhausted from his eight-day trip—which included visits to Belgrade, Madrid, and Lisbon—but he was also elated by what was clearly a personal success.[48]

The Eleventh Special Session

The same elements—the worsening global economic situation, the continuing energy crisis, Afghanistan, frustration over progress on the NIEO, the failure of UNIDO III, the question of U.S. leadership, Atlantic relations, congressional dislike of aid to the Third World, Third World radicalism, and the U.S. elections — were all present at the Eleventh Special Session of the General Assembly, which convened on August 25, 1980, in New York City to renew and to guide the world's commitment to international economic cooperation and development. For the world, the session would be part of what former Secretary of State Kissinger had called "a watershed," a "period of extraordinary creativity or a period when . . . the international order [could come] apart politically, economically and morally."[49] For the North-South dialogue, the meeting would be a benchmark; it would summarize progress to date on the NIEO and propose new programs for the eighties; it would mark the end of a decade of striving and hope and the beginning of another that would begin less with hope than with the promise, in the words of former Secretary Vance, of a new era of change, turbulence, and danger.

Most of the problems that faced the world at the beginning of the seventies — food, population, poverty, energy, finance, economic stability, and growth — were still present and were more grave than ever. The measure of the session's success would be whether its actions reflected lessons learned, whether it could forge a reasonable consensus, or whether it would continue a sterile stalemate. Although the special session agenda included the "Assessment of the Progress Made in the Establishment of the NIEO" and adoption of the new International Development Strategy, I shall concentrate on the global negotiations, because they were the lineal successor to the main line of negotiations on the NIEO that have been presented so far.[50]

For all the preparation, the story of the Eleventh Special Session is short and can be simply told. Although the country representatives filled the scheduled two weeks of plenary session with the usual speeches, members of the COW went to work on the basic structure of the global negotiations. Three or four days of work produced a short twelve-paragraph proposal on procedures and a time frame for the global negotiations. This proposal was referred to a smaller twenty-nation working group chaired by Canada, in which progress finally ground to a halt.

The unfinished proposal provided, inter alia, for a UN conference on international economic cooperation for development to meet at the UN headquarters in New York beginning on January 12, 1981, and lasting until September 1981. That conference would establish objectives and provide guidelines on the agenda items, indicate the time frame for negotiations, and entrust detailed negotiations to the specialized agencies and ad hoc groups where necessary. The conference would receive the results of the detailed negotiations with a view to reaching a "package agreement" with all parties committed to the implementation of that agreement. All agreements were to be reached by consensus.

The proposal was not much of a start compared to the session's aspirations, although some people thought any start was a hopeful sign and disagreements were useful in defining the issues. Because the Eleventh Special Session bogged down in preliminary procedural questions, the question of the substantive agenda was not even reached.[51]

The trouble lay in a basic conceptual difference in how the negotiations were to work, which, inevitably, found its focus in disputes over the choice of words. The problem centered around the relationship or division of labor between the central conference in New York and the specialized agencies. What was the proper role of the conference? Would it work from a neutrally worded agenda and develop general guidelines for the agencies? Or would it "instruct" the agencies, prejudging the issues in New York? Would the subsequent work of the agencies be accepted in New York and merely "coordinated" there? Or would the New York headquarters have the power to renegotiate? Where did the final authority on substance lie?

Behind the differences lay the G-77 predisposition to centralize power in New York. The United States did not want a central, *dirigiste,* managed system, preferring, as always, a pluralistic, decentralized system that would keep economic and political forums and issues well apart. The G-77 position carried to its logical extreme would outflank the authority and autonomy of the key institutions of the IBRD, IMF, and GATT by imposing G-77 control of their activities through the conference and, ultimately, the General Assembly. The United States was not only opposed to a centralized authority dominated by the G-77 but believed that it would not work. The pattern developing for the global negotiations, therefore, directly challenged a basic position maintained by the United States since the inception of the North-South dialogue. The point was underlined when Secretary-General Waldheim went over the heads of the U.S. delegation and appealed directly to President Carter to save the negotiations by agreeing to the majority view. Carter backed the delegation to the letter, which effectively brought the negotiations to an end.[52]

The United States maintained its position despite the fact that the other OECD countries — except for the United Kingdom and the Federal Republic of Germany — voted with the G-77. On the surface, the OECD countries would appear to have taken a "positive" stand. The facts of the situation, however, portray something less than principle and more like a desire for petty tactical advantage.

The European delegates to the United Nations in New York (especially the Nordics and the French) are subject to more constant political pressure than are delegates in Geneva and are more visible to their critical publics back home. Therefore, New York delegates have resisted the formation of a

Group B bloc, an action that gives them a wider scope for maneuver and less identification with the United States. They thus have the option of looking good in a Third World "beauty contest." At the Eleventh Special Session, the United States would obviously hold the line, so the other OECD countries could take a back seat. They believed, furthermore, that the "consensus" agreed to in the proposal would be a sufficient safeguard to block any objectionable developments. In any case, the real differences would be hammered out in substantive negotiations in Geneva where individual behavior could be cloaked within Group B.

In addition, Japan appeared, at long last, anxious to placate Third World opinion; Latin countries, e.g., Italy and France, are less inclined to take the verbiage of UN resolutions as commitments; and Canada escaped having to vote by chairing the working group. The result was that the negotiations were 90 percent a dialogue between the United States and the G-77, the United States appeared to be obstructionist and isolated in its obstruction, and Europe emerged untainted but protected all the same.[53]

Nor was the G-77 itself that well united. The threats and protestations of UNIDO III and the Havana Declaration failed to reappear as threatened. On the contrary, the G-77 appeared to be demoralized; it was certainly unhappy with the "gang of three" (United States, Federal Republic of Germany, and the United Kingdom—especially the United States) but not shrilly so. The OPEC countries, in spite of their rhetoric in support of global negotiations, had no real desire to have those international negotiations discuss OPEC policies on recycling or aid to non-OPEC LDCs. Nor were the OPEC countries any more anxious to have energy negotiated in New York than the United States was to have monetary affairs negotiated there. For the non-OPEC LDCs, the charade was wearing thin as escalating oil prices, inflation, debt, gross payments imbalances, and faltering development programs brought economic reality increasingly into relief. Latin America, especially, and Africa were skeptical that the global negotiations could achieve anything.[54]

In short, the Eleventh Special Session was a major nonevent. The NIEO assessment resulted in a report, which nobody read, and in some rhetoric, but it was not an issue. The global negotiations were referred to the regular session for further negotiation, presumably in November. Anxious that the special session not appear to have been a success, the G-77 had the agreed-upon International Development Strategy referred to the regular session for adoption.[55]

Widening the perspective a bit, I have suggested that the Eleventh Special Session would be a test case for U.S. policy, that it would reveal whether the rising perception of Third World strategic, political, and economic importance in the wake of Afghanistan might cause the United

States to alter its policy on the NIEO. In the event, the United States did not do so. Indeed, the United States, seeing before it a time of some turbulence and uncertainty, accentuated rather than modified its basic policy. It had gone into the negotiations positively and had played a more active role than any other country during the preparatory work in the COW, focusing on the four critical areas of food, energy, recycling, and protectionism and positive adjustment, which it believed were of top priority in both the near and the long term. It sent a high-level delegation to the Eleventh Special Session, including Secretary of State Muskie, U.S. Ambassador to the United Nations Donald F. McHenry, the senior officials involved in the North-South dialogue, and three members of Congress.[56] But, presented with the G-77 position on centralization in the actual negotiations, the United States realized that sooner or later it would have to take a stand and that it might as well do so at the beginning.

The terrors of being "isolated" in the United Nations no longer seemed so haunting, and the cutting edge of G-77 harrassment had been blunted by overuse. In view of the congressional inaction on the U.S. obligations to the IMF and the IBRD, what those institutions needed at the time was more rather than less support from the administration. Furthermore, the United States believed firmly that the health and progress of the Third World, as well as of the First World, depended on the proper functioning of those agencies.[57] Nor was the decision to stand firm merely a bureau-level decision. It had presidential backing and President Carter, in his address to the annual meeting of the IMF/IBRD on September 30 in Washington, again assured the agencies that "you must be confident that your decisions will not be determined or renegotiated in some other setting."[58]

This narrative thus ends, rudely perhaps, in the middle of the president's speech and, arbitrarily it would seem, during a pause between two rounds of ongoing negotiations. We stroll into the foyer wondering, What next? Will the global negotiations indeed take place? If so, will they achieve anything? Undersecretary Cooper has told us what to expect.

> We still hope that we can find a mutually acceptable formula which will allow global negotiations to get under way, and we are still hopeful that some positive results will emerge from such negotiations. We should make clear, however, that the critical issues . . . —such as energy development, food security, and an open trading system—must be dealt with whether or not we succeed in launching a global negotiating process. We will deal with these issues nationally, on a bilateral basis, and through multilateral agencies.[59]

The central question is not whether the negotiations will take place but, now as heretofore, what the United States intends to do about the problems that the dialogue purports to address. For, returning to the basic premise, the United States is the principal factor determining the direction and rate of progress. The most significant event of 1980, therefore, was not the desultory progress of the North-South dialogue but rather the rude awakening of the United States from its mood of withdrawal — its post-Vietnam experiment with global laissez-faire — and its efforts to resume a position of constructive leadership in the world. It is certainly too early to tell where those efforts might lead and what their implications for the North-South dialogue might be. For the moment, U.S. attention seems to be concentrated on defense, on East-West rather than on North-South concerns. The future of the global negotiations would not, therefore, appear to be very bright.

Toward Preservation of
the International Order

In this chapter I shall attempt to draw together the various elements treated thus far—the different interests, the fluctuations of those interests, the mechanism of policymaking, and the actual negotiation of the NIEO—to arrive at a coherent statement of what U.S. policy is and why. The assumption underlying this examination is that there is a fundamental coherence and meaning to this policy that links together the means and the objectives and that the policy must be seen in its totality to be understood. In other words, the policy is comprehensible if it is viewed as a process for achieving certain basic objectives. Because most scrutiny centers on a single event or a partial view, it usually leads to only a partial understanding that is negative or, worse, irrelevant. In point of fact, U.S. policy is fundamentally positive and supports the stated U.S. objectives. The necessary structure for an understanding of the policy therefore begins with the U.S. world view and U.S. interests.

Permanent U.S. Interests

In Chapter 1, I traced the evolution of U.S. policy during the early post–World War II years, beginning with the coherent world view presented in the Truman Doctrine and its subsequent implementing programs. That world view had three principal facets: maintenance of the open, free-market international economic order, resistance to Communist political and military intervention throughout the free world, and support for the newly emerging nations and assistance for their introduction into the international system. Those three interests provided the elements not only of a world view but also of a world system held together by a growing network of treaties, commitments, and institutions. I have traced, briefly, the working out of those interests and the policies that supported them through the decades of the fifties and sixties, as well as their affirmation by President Eisenhower and, especially, President Kennedy. U.S. participation in the North-South dialogue should be understood in the context of that world view and the responsibilities and commitments it has entailed.

During the decade of the seventies, the global system was subjected to severe threats because of the breakdown of the Bretton Woods system, the oil crisis, economic recession, Third World resurgence, and the steady growth of Soviet power, especially in the Third World. Simultaneously, the United States — defeated in Vietnam and suffering from domestic turmoil, a political crisis involving the presidency, and a disintegration of the national consensus — appeared to abandon its global commitments and to withdraw to an attitude of strictly national self-interest and nonintervention. President Carter was elected by a people more interested in domestic health than in the assumption of international responsibility, which Secretary Kissinger had tried to maintain through the troubled interregnum between the resignation of President Nixon in August 1974 and President Carter's assumption of office in January 1977.

The Third World campaign for the NIEO was profoundly affected by those events. The United States, as the major actor in the drama, dominated the negotiations and ultimately determined their outcome. But, because the United States was engrossed in divesting itself of the mantle of international responsibility and because the NIEO was presented to it in terms of an attack and a denunciation, its response was at first entirely negative. An attempt was made to change that response from confrontation to cooperation during the latter years of the Ford administration, but the results were nil and the goodwill collapsed on both sides. The Carter administration came to power with good intentions, recognizing the importance of Third World needs and demands, but its attention was soon diverted to concentrating on the dominating issues of SALT II, the Middle East peace negotiations, détente, China, economic recovery, oil, the war in Southeast Asia, the revolution in Iran, and a belated anxiety about Soviet and Cuban interventionism in Africa. Policy on the NIEO was relegated to the State Department bureaucracy, where the NIEO was treated as a nuisance issue and a potential threat to the international economic system. It was not until 1979 and the advent of UNCTAD V that Secretary Vance attempted a positive restatement of U.S. policy toward the Third World in general, including, by implication, the NIEO.

During 1979, the administration began to show signs that the decade of withdrawal, physical and psychological, was coming to an end and that President Carter had, perhaps, evolved from being a populist reformer to being a world statesman — or was trying to do so under the pressure of world events. In February, he spoke in Atlanta on "America's Role in a Turbulent World."[1] He talked about a "dangerous world," in which "freedom and democracy are still challenged," and reiterated the United

States' interest in maintaining global security, in sustaining a world trading and monetary system, and in helping new nations "so that each can develop its own future in independence and peace." Secretary Vance, speaking in Chicago on May 1, stressed the same elements.[2] "We are now living," he said, "in a period of history marked by deep and rapid change." He spelled out basic U.S. interests as being collective security for peace; maintenance of the open, nonprotectionist international economic system; and support for the "independence and diversity of the developing nations." The trend was confirmed by President Carter's State of the Union Address in January 1980, in which he stressed that the nation is no longer tempted by isolationism.

The significant aspect of those statements, however, is not so much that they marked a departure or change of mood from the record of the seventies but that in doing so they showed a remarkable consistency with the statements of U.S. interests of the previous decades, recalling another era of turmoil and the basic elements of the Truman Doctrine of 1947. The three elements of an open, free-market world trading system, political self-determination or independence and development for emerging countries, and defense against the challenge of Soviet communism may be regarded as forming the basic structure of U.S. foreign policy since World War II.

Those basic concepts are fundamental because they represent permanent national interests. They have been articulated in terms of the realities of life since 1946 and tested by experience. They have been accepted by the American people and the Congress, and they have not been seriously challenged since World War II. They are robust and seem to survive setbacks and challenges, both internal and external. Not every action or policy of the United States follows a set pattern, but over the decades, U.S. policy decisions can be seen as variations on a theme. Even after a decade of withdrawal, when stung into action, President Carter and his advisers put together a policy that was traditional and that had received the overwhelming approval of the Congress and acceptance of the American people. But it came too late. During the 1980 election campaign, Carter's original foreign policy of accommodation and détente came under vigorous attack, and he was loudly criticized, at home and abroad, for having been weak, vacillating, and indecisive.

Permanent Interests and the NIEO

Even though those U.S. interests and policies and the events that shaped them antedated the NIEO, they, nevertheless, made up the context that helped govern the U.S. response to the NIEO when it did appear on the world scene during the early seventies. The experience of the seventies, itself—when the world economic system seemed to be in grave peril and the United States in a mood of withdrawal—was also decisive in shaping the U.S. response; a further challenge to the world economic system from the Third World could only have been seen in the worst perspective. In understanding the U.S. response to the NIEO, therefore, it is essential to take all three of the basic interests into account; to do otherwise—to take U.S. relations with the Third World alone, which is what is usually done—is simplistic, misleading, and unprofitable. Furthermore, those national interests have special characteristics that significantly affect any U.S. policy toward the NIEO.

Because those U.S. policies represent permanent interests, they are apparently not subject to change either by external or even by internal influences. The United States has engaged in a long and sometimes ruthless struggle against international communism since World War II, with no significant alteration in the U.S. point of view. The United States forced an open, free-market economy on the world after the war and maintained U.S. leadership in promoting the reduction of trade barriers and maintaining openness in economic relations in spite of serious challenges from Germany (and Europe), Japan, and Third World exporting countries. The United States has not always been successful or fair, but its commitment has never wavered. The country initiated aid to emerging nations in 1950, and despite Congress's keeping aid on an annual basis, the program has continued and flourished. The question is not so much Why has the policy done so badly? but Why has it done as well as it has in the face of stiff opposition from U.S. business, much of Congress, and, increasingly, the electorate? Although rejecting the NIEO as a concept and facing massive public indifference, the Carter administration maintained a steady, positive commitment to the Third World and to an effective aid program. In other words, the U.S. policy of assistance to the Third World has a buoyancy that the opposition, whether from within or without, is seemingly unable to pierce.

It is the relationships among those three main interests rather than any outside influences that are important for North-South affairs. A comprehensive analysis of the interplay of the three variables over a period of thirty years is obviously beyond the scope of this book, but certain features that illustrate the point stand out. For example, in the competition for attention in Washington, security and economic interests clearly have had top priority, and Third World matters—development, global problems, the NIEO, etc.—have taken third place. Senator Moynihan spoke of this situation as "high and low politics." "In the postwar years," he wrote, U.S. diplomacy evolved

what has been called a dual tradition of high politics and low politics, with the curious incongruity that the high politics were concerned with death and the low politics merely with life. . . . High politics were security politics; weapons, wars and rumors of wars. Important matters.

By contrast, low politics, concerned with "social, humanitarian and cultural affairs," had suffered the ultimate indignity of not being regarded as politics at all by those who mattered.[3]

In other words, Third World affairs have not dominated, they have been dominated by economic and military priorities. That is the reason, familiar within the State Department, that it has been difficult to get adequate and sustained top-level attention directed toward the United Nations and other Third World economic and social affairs. Many a well-deserving proposal has been rejected or simply ignored because it had to compete with higher-priority security and economic problems.

There has also been a basic conflict between economic interests and development long before the NIEO, going back to the first aid bill in 1950. Business interests have been suspicious of and frequently opposed to government (including UN) intrusion into international economic life, and those interests have constituted the major opposition to "liberal" support for aid increases — except when such aid flowed back into business channels. Aid administrators have had to be careful that the taxpayers' money was not spent to develop industries in the Third World that might compete with U.S. business. In recent years, the trade unions reversed their historic stand in favor of aid and turned to protectionist policies to save workers from being undercut by cheap Third World imports.

When Third World development has prevailed over purely business considerations, it has been closely identified with defense against Soviet power or Communist subversion, a policy that largely characterized aid during the fifties. From the very beginning, aid has been justified on Capitol Hill largely on the grounds that by overcoming poverty and giving hope to millions of people in the Third World, the conditions under which communism flourishes can be eliminated. But even that reasoning has added to the rivalry for priority between business and development. According to the former, business means trade, jobs, and investment; free-market trade is the essence of capitalism; capitalism is the secret of prosperity; and prosperity is the ultimate defense against communism.

U.S. relations with the Third World are complex because many considerations are involved: self-determination and political independence, economic development, human rights, broad global issues, support for and relations with the UN system, security, international business, and bilateral relations. One of the consequences of the complexity and of the inevitable confusion is the charge that the United States has no Third World policy, or that what passes for policy is merely the surrogate for the promotion of U.S. commercial and financial interests. This charge may be understandable, but it is quite inaccurate.

In any discussion of the NIEO, what are thrust aside as irrelevant or simply overlooked are the very substantial U.S. programs that support Third World development and that antedate the NIEO by a quarter of a century. The current outlines of this Third World policy were set forth in Secretary Vance's speech in Seattle on March 30, 1979. It is not my purpose to give a detailed description of that policy, merely to note that it does exist, that it is important to the United States and the Third World, and that it has been substantial. The actual FY 1979 program amounted to a total of $13.8 billion, including $7.1 billion for economic assistance and $6.7 billion for military assistance (of which approximately $6 billion was for countries of the Near East). Specific economic programs included bilateral development programs, funds for international financial institutions, food aid, and refugee assistance.[4]

The United States also has a positive policy toward the Third World through the working of "the old international economic order." Although aid has become focused on the poorest countries, U.S. policy has been to use various trade and monetary measures to help the not-so-poor countries become viable members of the international economic order—a process of "graduation" from underdevelopment that countries such as South Korea, Mexico, and Brazil have experienced. The importance of the Third World in the economic order, although subject to some debate a decade ago, is now taken for granted, so that the issues of trading concessions, market access, industrial adjustment, Third World debt, and so forth are beginning to be major policy issues. This, not aid programs, is the basis for opposition to the NIEO by the United States and other DCs.

Although the Third World may have considerable grounds for criticism of the present economic order, it is incorrect to allege that that order is maintained, in the words of the Final Declaration of the Havana Summit, "by the exploitation of the labour as well as the transfer and plunder of the natural and other resources of the peoples of Africa, Asia, Latin America and other regions of the world."[5] Unfortunately, during discussions of the NIEO, especially by the ill-informed, only the problems are discussed, which results in a wholly one-sided picture.

Who Makes U.S. Policy?

Tracing how U.S. policy toward the NIEO is made and by whom in the U.S. government sharpens the focus of that policy and, as with the study of the negotiations, provides a concrete picture of what is otherwise merely a statement of national interest. That is to say, there is nothing abstract about the policies for they are reflected in and reinforced by the organization of government itself. Knowing, therefore, how U.S. policy is made and by whom provides, not just an exercise in institutional taxonomy, but the reality of what are otherwise words and declarations.

The Department of State is primarily responsible for the formulation, coordination, and implementation of policy on the NIEO. The State Department's responsibility and interest are not exclusive, but they are dominant. The only other agency with a strong influence is the Department of Treasury, which exercises a guiding hand over everything having to do with the international monetary system and exerts a generally conservative influence. The actual influence of the International Development Cooperation Agency (IDCA), established October 1, 1979, to coordinate U.S. government relations with the Third World, is yet to be determined, but it is likely that it will be limited to development policies and programs. President Carter came into office with good intentions but was himself dominated by pressing issues of international political and economic security to which Third World aspirations had to take second or third place. But a watching brief was maintained by the White House staff under Ambassador Henry Owen. Secretary Vance, reputed to have had a sympathetic interest in Third World problems, also suffered from having his time and attention preempted by crises and top priority issues, too much so to give his personal attention to the complex and detailed negotiations over the NIEO. Furthermore, he was not an economist and, like Secretary Kissinger, depended on trusted advisers who were.

Congressional interest in the North-South dialogue has dropped decisively since 1975–1976, when Congress supported U.S. participation in the Seventh Special Session, CIEC, and UNCTAD IV, to what may now be an all-time low.[6] The caustic denunciation of the United States at the Sixth Non-Aligned Summit (which got full coverage in the *Washington Post*) won no friends on Capitol Hill; neither has OPEC or the Ayatollah Khomeini. Senator Hubert Humphrey and Congressman Don Frazer, both strong advocates of a positive policy toward the Third World, are gone. The year 1980 was an election year, and domestic issues dominated. Congressmen who had backed SALT II and the Panama Canal Treaty believed they had already spent as much of the country's tolerance for "liberal" policies as they could; it was a conservative, Ronald Reagan, who reflected the mood of the country. It would be more to the point to say that during 1979–1980, congressional disinterest matured to active opposition.

Within the Department of State, policy during the Carter administration was dominated by Undersecretary of State for Economic Affairs Richard N. Cooper and by the assistant secretaries and staffs of the Bureau of Economic and Business Affairs (EB) and the Bureau of International

Organization Affairs (IO). Policy may be said to be the result of the competition between and the interaction of the two bureaus, subject, since January 1977, to the leadership and guidance of the economic undersecretary. Prior to that time, policy had been the result of only the competition between the two bureaus. That change is not unimportant, for it is the bureaus that provide the continuity for policy from administration to administration, and those two bureaus are depended on to articulate, administer, and negotiate the policy. It may even be said that it is the bureaucracy, not the administration, that actually makes the policy — or that the policy is now a reflection of the vested institutional or bureaucratic interests rather than the other way around. Therefore, it is very much in terms of the responsibilities, workings, attitudes, personnel, and relationships of those two bureaus that U.S. policy on the NIEO has evolved.

The Bureau of International Organization Affairs (IO)

The Bureau of International Organization Affairs of the Department of State has traditionally had primary responsibility in the government for U.S. participation in the United Nations and its specialized agencies. For many years, this responsibility also meant that IO had primary responsibility for multilateral relations with the Third World, a function it carried out with very little interest or serious interference from other agencies of the government. These relations should be differentiated from the equally — perhaps even more — important but less publicized bilateral relations, which are conducted by area bureaus, e.g. Africa and Latin America, with desks for each country, and from the Agency for International Development (AID), which has a parallel "desk" and a regional bureau structure organized on a bilateral basis.

Over the years, IO acquired a long institutional memory and a sophistication concerning Third World issues, organizations, and movements not found elsewhere in the Department of State or even, perhaps, in Washington. IO directed, or at least coordinated, U.S. policy toward most international organizations, managed U.S. participation in international conferences, and prepared instructions for U.S. delegations. It was the first bureau to be involved in the new global issues — outer space, Antarctica, human rights, environment, population, food, health, and education.

IO therefore tended to take global, generally more "liberal," and nonpolitical views of many problems. It early recognized the power and importance of the Third World and the need for industrialized countries to accommodate Third World demands. That was the bureau's job, and IO has attracted to it progressive thinkers like Harlan Cleveland, Richard Gardner, and Charles Maynes.

The bureau also has had responsibility for managing U.S. assessed and voluntary contributions to the United Nations, specialized agencies, and various development funds and for defending the budget requests for those expenditures to Congress. The U.S. share of UN assessed budgets dropped from 40 percent in 1946 to 25 percent over the last decade, but, because of the rapid growth of the UN system, the absolute amount has increased in sizable increments each year. The UN regular budget has been increasing annually at rates of 20 percent to 25 percent. The 1979 UN budget of $1.1 billion was about 30 percent of the total cost of operations for the first twenty-five years ($3.9 billion). The U.S. bill for assessed and voluntary contributions to the United Nations and specialized agencies increased from $553 million in 1977 to $645 million for 1979, not including $50 million for peacekeeping and refugee relief.[7]

Managing a small budget can be done without too much scrutiny or criticism. Managing a billion-dollar biennial budget cannot. Indeed, the UN budget attracts — and this is the point — more attention from Congress, the General Accounting Office (GAO), and the Office of Management and Budget (OMB) than do the substantive UN issues. As UN budgets have bloated over the years, one of the most critical functions of IO has become budget management, which tends profoundly to temper the traditional liberal policy toward the North-South dialogue. U.S. delegates to international conferences may have considerable latitude on substantive matters, but on budgets, organization, and administration the department's instructions are firm and unequivocal: "Hold the line."

Bureau of Economic and Business Affairs (EB)

Ten years ago, the top staff members of the State Department were almost exclusively political, and in diplomacy, the political line had always had clear primacy over the economic, administrative, or consular lines. That is no longer the case. During the seventies, the Bureau of Economic and Business Affairs (EB), or the E Bureau as it is called, emerged as one of the most competent and powerful bureaus in the State Department as international economic problems — oil, monetary affairs, and trade — surged to the top of the international agenda. Much of the credit must go to one man, former Assistant Secretary Julius L. Katz, who developed the E Bureau from a middle-echelon to a top-drawer organization, so that when the era of global problems arose during the seventies, the E Bureau was able to rise to the challenge. It carried weight and had respect and had earned both. The bureau had mastered the increasingly complex economic agenda, which political officers only vaguely understand.

EB interest in the North-South problems and UN affairs was minimal prior to the 1973 oil crisis. However, with the oil embargo and the launching of the NIEO, its interest grew because the primary economic interests of the United States were being overtly challenged. Trade in commodities and manufactures, fuels and energy, and international finance were EB responsibilities. The World Food Conference in 1974 impinged on grain markets and food policy, both aspects of commodity policy and trade. An internal struggle ensued between IO, responsible for UN affairs, and EB, responsible for commodities and food policy. EB won. IO had been responsible for preparations for the Sixth Special Session of the General Assembly in April 1974, but by April 1975, the Assistant Secretary for Economic and Business Affairs, Thomas O. Enders, was firmly in charge of preparations for the Seventh Special Session. EB has dominated policy at the bureau level ever since.

That dominance has had a crucial impact on U.S. policy toward the NIEO. The bureau's primary responsibility, irrespective of the NIEO, is support for U.S. economic and business interests and of the open, free-market economy and its institutions — one of the principal and nonnegotiable pillars of U.S. foreign policy. The basic attitude of the bureau toward the NIEO, therefore, has ranged from hostility to grudging tolerance, with the firm belief that economic "common sense" would prevail over Third World loyalty to its own ideology. The principal U.S. negotiators and policymakers concerned with North-South conferences since the Seventh Special Session have been officials of the E Bureau, and their primary mission has been to foster the present economic order, not to subvert it. IO still bears primary responsibility for UN matters and maintains a generally more liberal attitude toward Third World demands, but it can go no further than EB is prepared to go.

Undersecretary of State for Economic Affairs

When the Carter administration assumed office in January 1977, Richard N. Cooper became Undersecretary of State for Economic Affairs, the fourth most powerful post in the Department of State reporting directly to the secretary. He was given responsibility for North-South relations, and Secretary Vance, distracted by crisis management, left those matters in his hands. Cooper was the umpire between IO and EB but he usually came down on the side of economic reality. Although no ideologist, he distrusted government intervention in the economy, grand schemes and objectives, and bureaucratic management. He believed that the health of the international economy was the best assurance of LDC growth, and he was particularly protective of the IMF and what he conceived to be its proper role. In short, Cooper was a pragmatist concerned with solving each problem as it arose, mainly along market economy lines. He believed that aspects of the NIEO violated basic economics and that in cases such as redeployment governments should keep out and let the economy bring about change.

Thus U.S. policy on the NIEO during the Carter administration was largely made by Cooper, C. Fred Bergsten (former Treasury assistant secretary for international affairs), Robert Hormats (former deputy assistant secretary of state for economic and business affairs), and Ambassador Henry Owen, with Cooper primus inter pares. That group, constantly in touch and in close collaboration with senior officials of IO, made the basic decisions on strategy and policy.

Negotiating the NIEO

By challenging, wittingly or unwittingly, one of the basic interests of the United States, the NIEO brought into being a powerful and competitive group, with its own ideas and objectives, that was not inclined to compromise with untested alternatives. The counter offer to the LDCs has been the open, free-market international economic order, in which LDCs can move upward through a process of "graduation" — which was denounced at Arusha and Havana but has already produced a new generation of "nearly industrialized countries" (NICS), e.g., Brazil, Mexico, Taiwan, and South Korea, which are increasingly able to fend for themselves.

Chapter 4 was devoted to an analysis of the negotiations in order to identify more exactly what was actually going on and to discover the real issues in dispute. It will be recalled, therefore, that the United States strongly supported certain aspects of the program — basic needs, ECDC, and technology transfer — and opposed others. Although the United States actually has supported in its own programs most of the ultimate economic and social objectives of Third World development, it has rejected the means and methods by which the Third World seeks to bring those changes about: more international management, new institutions and new funds, increased bureaucracy, a dilution of the authority of the present system, and interference with the free-market system. In other words, on the negotiating level, the differences were not so much a conflict over social and economic objectives as over the international economic system — how it works, who pays for it, who takes the risks, and, ultimately, who controls it.

Thus, the actual negotiations on the NIEO directly challenge one of the permanent U.S. interests, which is historically resistant to change from within or without. To give in to the NIEO would be as unthinkable for the United States as turning Western collective security over to Eastern Europe. Ironically, the NIEO has drawn the most liberal bureau, IO, into an alliance with the E Bureau (with which it is ordinarily at philosophic odds) by demanding at every turn new funds and institutions to be paid for by the West. IO, also responsible for budget management, must oppose those demands. In other words, the NIEO strategy — by concentrating on new institutions, new funds, and new bureaucracies — brought the two bureaus — ordinarily opposed to each other philosophically — into joint opposition; the one for policy reasons, the other for administrative reasons. Backing up those bureaus have been a negative Congress, a conservative Treasury, a preoccupied administration, and a largely indifferent people.

Looking Ahead

It may be concluded that U.S. policy toward the international economic system has been coherent and consistent. It has been a standard pillar of U.S. foreign policy and a major fact of international life since 1945. It has been assiduously maintained on all levels, from institution-building to detailed negotiations, and has emerged with the most authority in successive rounds of trade liberalization, economic cooperation (mainly through the OECD community), and monetary and financial measures. From the point of view of the United States, this policy has been positive, sensible, economic, and justified by results.

Unfortunately, that policy has acquired an almost totally negative image as far as the Third World is concerned, which sees the international economic system as the author of its own ills. Since the Third World view is the one expressed by most UN agencies, by the media (if at all), and by voluntary agencies, the positive aspect is lost behind a barrage of partisan protest. That there are grounds for criticism cannot be denied. The world is changing; there are abuses and inequities. But, as for understanding and dealing with the policies of the major factor in international economic affairs, the criticism is not particularly useful since it invokes no realistic alternative.

What about the future? The influence of the decade of the seventies on U.S. policy and how the United States, in a defensive posture, reacted against the NIEO have been described. Since Afghanistan, the United States seems to have emerged from its mood of isolationism and to have resumed a more positive, responsible attitude toward world events and global problems. A post-Afghanistan increase in a U.S. awareness of the strategic and economic importance of certain Third World countries has also been noted. Might not these significant perceptual and attitudinal changes produce a change in U.S. policy toward the NIEO? The Eleventh Special Session's deliberations on global negotiations were looked at as the test case.

In the event, there has been no change in U.S. policy whatsoever. At the Eleventh Special Session, the United States decided to make a stand, not to provide more concessions. The reasons are rather obvious. Afghanistan had come as yet another challenge, another threat to political and economic security. The economic system itself continued to be in serious difficulty—perceived as the result mainly of OPEC policies—with no relief in sight. So the basic U.S. reaction was again defensive: with regard to Afghanistan, increased military capability; with regard to energy, delinking energy and growth or, in other words, more self-sufficiency through alternative energy sources and conservation; with regard to trade, stronger pressures for protection from competitive imports and an export drive. With regard to the NIEO, the U.S. reaction resulted not in more economic concessions or commitments to expensive schemes for international management but in a desire to hold the line. That fact illustrates the thesis that the U.S. commitment to support the present international economic order is a permanent and nonnegotiable facet of U.S. foreign policy, not readily subject to significant change by external or even by internal events.

With regard to aid, the Reagan administration has already taken much of the guesswork out of the future. The new administration has promised not massive transfers but massive cutbacks in the aid budget, including reductions of aid to the least developed countries and of contributions to MDBS, UN agencies, the IDA, and Food for Peace. Bigger defense budgets have been promised, making development assistance subsidiary to military aid and giving priority over multilateral aid to bilateral aid to those countries that are of "key importance to the U.S."[8]

With those abrupt proposals, the Reagan administration brought an end to whatever illusions might have survived from the administration of President Carter. No doubt modifications will set in as the consequences become more readily apparent. However, the prospects for significant change, during the next four years at least, would appear to be slight. The new leadership has clearly perceived U.S. self-interest in terms of military and economic defense. Innovative proposals to change the international economic order or to provide concessions to Third World countries are likely to fall on barren ground.

Conclusions

This volume began with two principal concerns. One was to determine whether the North-South negotiations are an effective medium for finding solutions to the global problems of food, population, energy, poverty, development, environment, and so forth, all of which are of profound importance to the future of the world as a whole. Second was to determine whether the U.S. policy in this process has been supportive of U.S. interests. The conclusions that can be reached follow.

With regard to U.S. policy, there can be no doubt that it has served the classic U.S. interest of maintaining the open, free-market international economic order against Third World efforts to change it. The State Department has ably defended this interest, both on the conceptual level and at the negotiating table, and promoted it in the wider area of economic relations, with DCs and LDCs alike.

However, that interest has been defended and promoted at serious political cost. The NIEO is at once a prescription for the future and the product of poverty, subordination, frustration, and humiliation. The NIEO is the attempt, in the declaration's words, to achieve real independence, equity, and justice. So, although it may purport to be an economic program, it is also, increasingly, a political reality. The flat refusal of the United States to recognize the NIEO as a legitimate program has therefore generated a legacy of frustration and ill will and has eroded the reputation of the United States throughout the Third World.

The consequence for U.S. strategic interests has also been corrosive. With the Soviet Union in an increasingly aggressive posture and with a return to bipolarity and Cold War psychology, it is no advantage to the United States to have antagonized Third World countries, which control essential resources, strategic real estate, and vital shipping lanes.

With regard to global problem solving, the North-South dialogue has made no great achievements. It has publicized issues and educated the world, both governmental and nongovernmental, concerning the problems and the difficulties of finding solutions to them. However, progress now seems stalled because of a basic disagreement over how to address the problem. The North is usually blamed for "intransigence," and the South, for "lack of realism," but perhaps some of the reasons for the disagreement can be found in the negotiating process itself.

1. Neither the NIEO nor the present international economic system is negotiable. Five years of trying have shown that. Unless some of the factors change substantially, further negotiations will probably be fruitless as well. Emphasis should be concentrated, therefore, on discovering possible areas of accommodation. Part of the problem has been that the G-77 has failed to understand or to accept that the U.S. government could not, even if it were so disposed, negotiate away the free-enterprise system. The present system may not be a pure free-market one — no one would claim that — but neither will the governments of the industrialized countries — even if it were in their power to do so — consider turning the economic system over to Third World management along Third World lines. What the U.S. negotiators have failed to understand is that a basic needs program or unilateral offers are no substitute for the NIEO. The G-77 has been explicit about that. The U.S. negotiators should not, therefore, be surprised or offended if such U.S. offers do not "improve the tone of the dialogue." Under the circumstances, the so-called dialogue, as has frequently been observed, is more like two monologues.

2. Negotiations of the NIEO in the usual open-ended UN forum are admirably suited to keeping results to a minimum. Sheer numbers guarantee that a consensus will be on the level of the lowest common denominator. Former Jamaican Prime Minister Michael Manley has complained:

> Now when you have about 150 sovereign entities lined up on opposite sides you already have a difficult negotiating exercise. Each side finds it extremely difficult to actually negotiate because each side is so large and subject to so many different types of decision-making [*sic*] processes. The result is that negotiations get bound to the pace of the slowest in the process.[1]

That situation plays into the hands of "conservatives," who are only too willing to see the NIEO deteriorate into a welter of toothless resolutions and meetings.

3. On the negotiating level, the NIEO is literally a paper tiger. Even though real issues of great import are involved — of profound interest to the community of nations as a whole and its individual members, North and South — the actual dialogue is but a pale image of the real thing. As many a knowledgeable observer has complained, the results of the North-South resolutions are not changes in the social or economic order but, rather, what have become surrogates for change — a swelling system of resolutions,

conferences, committees, and bureaucracies.

4. A basic problem of the negotiations is that the demands of one side and the concessions of the other have been unbalanced. That situation has a certain logic in the Third World's view, which is that today's concessions are a long overdue payment or reparations for past exploitation. However, to the North the process has looked more like a court of justice than a diplomatic negotiation. It might be worthwhile to try to conduct a negotiation on the basis of balanced demands on both sides.

5. There should be general agreement before any specific negotiation begins on what the North-South negotiations are all about. The South insists on treating the international order as a whole and has vast plans for restructuring major sectors of the system worldwide, more or less simultaneously; the United States and Group B insist on negotiating each problem separately on a piecemeal basis. The South sees the issues as basically political; the North, as economic. As Indian Ambassador to CIEC K. G. Vaidya has concluded, nothing substantial will be achieved until the negotiators get down to fundamentals.[2]

The third conclusion is that the North-South dialogue is already out of date, economically and politically. The NIEO and its supporting programs and declarations were a response to the problems of the fifties and the sixties, during which time development was associated with economic growth, especially in the industrialized sector. However, because of the outbreak of systemic crises and the awareness of threats to the environment, of escalating population pressures, and of resource shortages, the decade of the seventies ushered in a new era of global problems. With those new problems came the sobering realization that the overwhelming reality about the world economic system is that the era of rapid growth, North and South, is coming to an end. Still to be faced and just over the horizon is the demand for employment for the millions of Third World youth now approaching maturity. The economic and social developments have not eroded the North-South perspective, since many of the problems assume their most intense form as LDC problems. However, the priorities of the future will not be the same as those of the sixties. The nations of the world are presented, in effect, with a modern dilemma with which they are not even close to coping. They are trying to solve national problems through economic growth and development while moving inexorably into an era of worldwide shortages and limited growth; they are faced with the grim prospect of a zero-sum world in which the size of the pie remains the same, and only the size of the shares can be varied.

Since the beginning of the seventies, the integrity of the international system, political as well as economic, appears to be increasingly at risk: first, as we have seen, economically because of monetary disorder, oil price increases, inflation, and recession; then, less clearly perceived, because of the increasing hostility in North-South relations. Meanwhile, overshadowing all other considerations, there is the emergence of the Soviet Union as a global power and a threatening one at that. These conflicts and problems, mounting during a decade of declining U.S. power, influence, and authority, present a serious challenge to the political security of the West. The deterioration of the West's political relations with the Third World over the North-South dialogue should be seen in this context and not just as the unfortunate by-product of economic self-defense.

In summary, the issues being addressed by the North-South dialogue are basic and important to the world, both North and South, whether they are thought of as North-South issues or as global issues. Their intrinsic importance has been heightened by the crises of the seventies and the severe strains that have been put upon the economic and political structures of the world system. These strains will probably intensify with time. The best possible resolution of the problems is therefore a matter of high priority. The North-South dialogue, however, which purports to address at least some of the problems, shows little sign of making any further progress and, unless things change significantly, probably will not do so. Certain negotiating problems that have been responsible, at least in part, for the stalemate have been indicated. It has also been suggested that the agenda and objectives of the North-South dialogue, including U.S. policy and tactics, are out of date and increasingly irrelevant in terms of the long-range economic and political realities.

The fourth and final conclusion, therefore, is in the form of a recommendation. That is, that a new initiative, appropriate to the realities ahead and to the gravity of the issues, be undertaken. The NIEO is not the answer, but it is a symptom of the times, of the glaring asymmetries in the world system, and of the need for change. The report and some of the recommendations of the Brandt Commission, including its call for a North-South summit, could be a beginning. But the outcome all depends on the United States. Because of its preponderant influence, the United States must take the initiative and assume a creative, partnership role. U.S. policies must also have a new world view and a long-range orientation if the economic, strategic, and political challenges of the next quarter century are to be effectively met. The publication of the *Global 2000* report to the president and the establishment of a task force to produce recommendations for action are hopeful signs.[3] Still to come must be a new sense of responsibility, self-confidence, and moral authority, which were abandoned somewhere along the way and have been wholly lacking in the context of the North-South negotiations.

The new U.S. administration and the mood of the country following the Iranian hostage crisis suggest that the United States will be more confident and self-assertive in the months and years ahead, that it will genuinely strive to resume a leadership role. It remains to be seen whether that will to power will be accompanied by the requisite vision, the diplomatic imagination, and the willingness, in the words of former Secretary Muskie, to bear the costs of leadership.

Notes

Chapter 1

1. William Roger Louis, *Imperialism at Bay* (Oxford: Oxford University Press, 1977), pp. 199–200.

2. Walter LaFeber, *America, Russia, and the Cold War 1945*–1975, 3rd ed. (New York: John Wiley and Sons, 1976), p. 12.

3. Ibid., pp. 51–52.

4. Ibid., p. 52.

5. Dean Acheson, *Present at the Creation* (London: Hamish Hamilton, 1970), pp. 220–225; LaFeber, op. cit., pp. 50–57.

6. Congressional Research Service, *The Soviet Union and the Third World: A Watershed in Great Power Conflict,* Report to the Committee on International Relations, House of Representatives (Washington, D.C.: Government Printing Office, 1977).

7. LaFeber, op. cit., p. 156.

8. Peter Willetts, *The Non-Aligned Movement* (London: Frances Pinter, 1978), and A. W. Singham, ed., *The Non-Aligned Movement in World Politics* (Westport, Conn.: Lawrence Hill & Co., 1977).

9. John F. Kennedy, Inaugural Address, January 1961.

10. LaFeber, op. cit., p. 235.

11. William Ashworth, *A Short History of the International Economy Since 1850,* 3rd ed. (London: Longmans, 1975), chap. 10.

12. Ibid., p. 299.

13. Henry Brandon, *The Retreat of American Power* (London: Bodley Head, 1972), p. 239.

14. LaFeber, op. cit., pp. 280–281.

15. Edward R. Fried and Charles L. Shultze, eds., *Higher Oil Prices and the World Economy* (Washington, D.C.: Brookings Institution, 1975), p. 11.

16. Development Assistance Committee, "Development Cooperation 1975," Report by the chairman (Paris: OECD, 1975), p. 37.

17. Louis Turner and Mary Hargreaves, "Energy as a Central Factor," *Europe and the North-South Dialogue,* ed. Wolfgang Wessels, Atlantic Papers no. 35 (Paris: Atlantic Institute for International Affairs, 1978), p. 27.

18. Roger D. Hansen and Staff of Overseas Development Council, "The U.S. and World Development: A Year of Opportunity," in *The U.S. and World Develop-*

ment: Agenda for Action, 1976 (New York: Praeger, 1976), p. 2.

19. Michael Hudson, *Global Fracture* (New York: Harper & Row, 1977), p. 87.

20. George Ball, *Diplomacy for a Crowded World* (London: Bodley Head, 1976), p. 338.

21. Turner and Hargreaves, op. cit., p. 28.

22. Roger D. Hansen, "Major U.S. Options on North-South Relations: A Letter to President Carter," in John W. Sewell and Staff of the Overseas Development Council, *The U.S. and World Development: Agenda for Action, 1977*, (New York: Praeger, 1977), p. 28.

23. Willetts, op. cit., pp. 26-29.

24. Cairo Preparatory Meeting June 6-12 and Belgrade First Summit September 1-6, 1961.

25. Hansen, op. cit., p. 28.

26. W. Howard Wriggins and Gunnar Adler-Karlsson, *Reducing Global Inequities* (New York: McGraw Hill, 1978), p. 68.

27. Ibid., p. 69.

28. United Nations, *UN Yearbook 1974* (New York: UN Office of Publications Information, 1977), vol. 28, p. 306.

29. Wriggins and Adler-Karlsson, op. cit., p. 69.

30. Congressional Research Service, op. cit., pp. 86-91.

31. Quoted in James W. Howe and Staff of the Overseas Development Council, *The U.S. and World Development: Agenda for Action, 1975* (New York: Praeger, 1975), p. 2.

Chapter 2

1. Roger D. Hansen, *Beyond the North-South Stalemate* (New York: McGraw-Hill, 1979), p. 25.

2. W. Tapley Bennett, Jr., "Report of the U.S. Delegation to the Second General Conference of the UN Industrial Development Organization (UNIDO)," Lima, Peru, March 12-27, 1975 (Washington, D.C.: 1975), p. 1.

3. Ibid., p. 2.

4. Roger D. Hansen and Staff of Overseas Development Council, *The U.S. and World Development: Agenda for Action, 1976* (New York: Praeger, 1976), p. 2.

5. Hon. Thomas O. Enders, U.S. Ambassador to the European Communities interview, February 6, 1980.

6. Philip H. Trezise, *The Atlantic Connection* (Washington, D.C.: Brookings Institution, 1975), p. 1.

7. Daniel P. Moynihan, *A Dangerous Place* (London: Secker & Warburg, 1979), p. 121.

8. Henry Kissinger, "The Global Challenge and International Cooperation," Speech given in Milwaukee, Wisconsin, July 14, 1975 (*Department of State Bulletin*, August 4, 1975, pp. 149-157).

9. Bhashkar P. Menon, *Global Dialogue: The New International Order* (Oxford: Pergamon Press, 1977), p. 6.

10. Daniel P. Moynihan, "The United States in Opposition," in *The First World, The Third World,* ed. Karl Brunner (Rochester, N.Y.: University of Rochester, 1978), pp. 105–132.

11. Henry Kissinger, "Global Consensus and Economic Development," Speech to Seventh Special Session, September 1, 1975 (*Department of State Bulletin,* September 22, 1975, pp. 425–441).

12. Hansen and Staff of ODC, op. cit., p. 57.

13. Moynihan, *A Dangerous Place,* pp. 131–132.

14. Ibid., p. 133.

15. Hansen and Staff of ODC, op. cit., p. 5.

16. Enders interview.

17. Moynihan, *A Dangerous Place,* pp. 131–139.

18. Menon, op. cit., pp. 8–13.

19. UN, General Assembly, Resolution 3342 (S-VII) was essentially a compromise between the most extreme demands of the NIEO and the hitherto negative attitude of the United States.

20. Menon, op. cit., p. 37.

21. Jahangir Amuzegar, "A Requiem for the North-South Conference," *Foreign Affairs* (October 1977), p. 136.

22. Jonathan Carr, "The Position of the European Community," in *Europe and the North-South Dialogue,* ed. Wolfgang Wessels, Atlantic Papers no. 35 (Paris: Atlantic Institute for International Affairs, 1978), p. 24.

23. K. G. Vaidya, "The Paris Episode in the North-South Dialogue" (Paper written for Centre for Research on the New International Economic Order, Oxford, June 2, 1979), p. 33. Vaidya was ambassador and leader of the Indian delegation to the CIEC.

24. Menon, op. cit., pp. 19–23.

25. Henry Kissinger, "UNCTAD IV: Expanding Cooperation for Global Economic Development," Address to UNCTAD IV, Nairobi, May 6, 1976 (*Department of State Bulletin,* May 31, 1976, pp. 657–672).

26. Ibid.

27. Paul H. Boeker, "Report of U.S. Delegation to the United Nations Conference on Trade and Development, Fourth Session, Nairobi, Kenya, May 5–31, 1976" (Washington, D.C.: 1976), p. 3.

28. Ibid., pp. 55–56.

29. Ibid., pp. 57–59.

30. UNCTAD, press release, April 18, 1977 (Geneva: Information Service, TAD/INF/869).

31. Shridath S. Ramphal, "The North-South Dialogue," *Third World Quarterly* 1:1 (January 1979), p. 11.

32. Boeker, op. cit., Appendix 4, p. 2. The privately expressed opinions of the U.S. negotiators about the Common Fund are emphatic and critical.

33. Richard N. Cooper, "Department Discusses Results of CIEC Meeting," *Department of State Bulletin,* July 18, 1977, p. 96.

34. Ibid.

35. *Guardian,* December 11, 1978, p. 16.

36. Ibid.

37. John J. Harter, press release, December 23, 1978 (Washington, D.C.: IPS, EUR-71).

38. Ibid.

39. Enders interview.

Chapter 3

1. Shridath S. Ramphal, Commonwealth secretary-general, personal interview, Marlborough House, London, January 11, 1979. The Arusha meeting was sponsored by the Third World Foundation, London.

2. *Guardian,* December 20, 1978. An earlier report had quoted Ramphal as saying: "The age of polite dialogue with developed countries is over and the phase of organized pressure should begin. . . . The North is unlikely to be shaken out of its complacency unless its vital interests are threatened or the South gets better organized" (*Guardian,* December 18, 1978). The December 20 story in the *Guardian* printed a "clarification" that those views had been wrongly attributed to Ramphal. Nevertheless, they prefigured the twin channels of future effort, self-reliance and "pressure" tactics.

3. Altaf Gauhar, "Editor's Note," *Third World Quarterly* 1:1 (January 1979), p. v.

4. Shridath S. Ramphal, "The North-South Dialogue," *Third World Quarterly* 1:1 (January 1979), p. 13.

5. Ramphal interview. Cooper was U.S. undersecretary of state for economic affairs, appointed by Carter in 1977.

6. Dr. Dale Hathaway, U.S. assistant secretary of agriculture and U.S. delegate to IWC Preparatory Group First Meeting September 28–October 7, 1977, PREP (77) 8, September 30, 1977.

7. James Parker, member of U.S. delegation to IWA Conference, personal interview, U.S. embassy, London, April 1979.

8. Ibid. Note the paradoxical situation in which producers favor reserve arrangements during years of surplus and oppose them when they are most needed during years of shortage. Importers react in opposite fashion; they benefit from low prices during surplus years and favor reserves during years of shortages. Thus, at any given time, importers and exporters find themselves in opposite positions. This situation inevitably ensures that the exporters' policies will be characterized as self-serving, and their concessions, as grudging. It also ensures that Third World demands will be hysterical during years of shortage and short-sighted during times of plenty. The secret, according to one State Department official, is to negotiate when the market is halfway between the two extremes.

9. International Wheat Council, "Eighty-sixth Session and Conference," press release, March 23, 1979 (London: CL 86/15); for draft text, see UNCTAD, TD/Wheat. 6/R. 5 (February 19, 1979).

10. Department of Agriculture, official source, February 1979.

11. U.S. Information Service, press release, February 9, 1979 (Geneva: USIS, FC/30).

12. UNCTAD, "Arusha Programme for Collective Self-Reliance and Framework for Negotiations," TD/236 (Geneva: May 1979), p. 1. Note that UNCTAD V was held only three years rather than the usual four years after UNCTAD IV. This change was made to break the unfortunate timing of UNCTAD conferences with U.S. election years.

13. Ibid., Annex II, pp. 1-9.

14. Ibid., Annex II, p. 6.

15. Ibid., Annex II, pp. 11-13.

16. Ibid., p. 5.

17. Gamani Corea, "Notification," Letter to UNCTAD members, TDO 254/2 (Geneva: UNCTAD, January 29, 1979).

18. U.S., Mission, Geneva, official source, January 1979.

19. UNCTAD, "Arusha Programme," pp. 36-38.

20. U.S. Embassy, London, "U.S. Goals in the Common Fund Negotiations," press release, March 3, 1979 (London: ICA).

21. U.S., Mission, Geneva, "U.S. Heartened by Common Fund Agreement," press release, March 20, 1979 (Geneva: EURX-2).

22. *Guardian,* March 21, 1979.

23. Iain Guest, *Guardian,* April 9, 1979.

24. *Economist,* "Mountain in Labor," March 24, 1979.

25. U.S., Mission, Geneva, official source, March 1979.

26. U.S., Mission, Geneva, "Conference Agrees on Fundamental Elements of a Common Fund," press release, March 20, 1979 (Geneva: EURX-4).

27. Joel Johnson, member of Policy Planning Staff, Department of State, personal letter, November 28, 1979. Johnson was primarily responsible for drafting and coordinating policy on Vance's Seattle speech.

28. Jimmy Carter, "America's Role in a Turbulent World," Department of State *Current Policy Series* no. 57 (Washington, D.C.: March 1979).

29. Johnson letter.

30. Cyrus Vance, "America's Commitment to Third World Development," *Secretary of State,* March 30, 1979.

31. *Financial Times,* April 4, 1979.

32. Cyrus Vance, "Meeting the Challenge of a Changing World," press release, May 2, 1979 (London: International Communications Agency).

33. James Reston, column, *International Herald Tribune,* May 5-6, 1979.

Chapter 4

1. Independent Commission on International Development Issues (ICIDI), *North-South: A Programme for Survival* (London: Pan Books, 1980), p. 1.

2. For a good discussion of negotiating the Common Fund, see Robert L. Rothstein, *Global Bargaining: UNCTAD and the Quest for a New International Economic Order* (Princeton, N.J.: Princeton University Press, 1979).

3. This generalized summary of the NIEO is based on a wide variety of sources, both formal and informal. Basic sources are UN, General Assembly, "Declaration

on the Establishment of a New International Economic Order, the Programme of Action," Resolution 3201 (S-IV) (New York: May 1, 1974), and "The Charter of Economic Rights and Duties of States (CERDS)," Resolution 3281 (XXIX) (New York: December 12, 1974); UNCTAD, "Arusha Programme for Collective Self-Reliance and Framework for Negotiations" (Geneva: February 28, 1979); and Non-Aligned Countries, "Final Declaration," Conference of Heads of State or Government of Non-Aligned Countries, Conf. 6/C.2 Doc.1/Rev.3 (Havana: September 3–9, 1979).

4. UNCTAD, "Arusha Programme," Annex II, p. 6.

5. Department of State, "Background Information," (Washington, D.C.: April 30, 1979), item 8. (Unclassified position papers prepared for each substantive item of the agenda for UNCTAD V.)

6. UNCTAD, "Evaluation of the World Trade and Economic Situation," TD/224 (Geneva: March 28, 1979).

7. The final act of the UN Conference on Trade and Employment, 1948, which led to abortive efforts to establish an International Trade Organization (ITO).

8. UNCTAD, "Policy Issues in the Fields of Trade, Finance, and Money and Their Relationship to Structural Change at the Global Level," TD/225 (Geneva: April 11, 1979).

9. UNCTAD, "Arusha Programme," pp. 25–29.

10. Department of State, op. cit., item 8.

11. Official U.S. source, June 1979. An illustration of the endemic rivalry between the G-77 establishment in New York and that in Geneva.

12. Ibid.

13. UN Information Center, press release, June 18, 1979 (London: BR/79/22).

14. Official U.S. source, June 1979.

15. OECD, "UNCTAD Fifth Session," CES/UN(79) 15 (Paris: June 13, 1979), p. 1.

16. Ibid., p. 11.

17. UNCTAD, "Implications for Developing Countries of the New Protectionism in Developed Countries," TD/226 (Geneva: March 6, 1979).

18. UNCTAD, "Arusha Programme," pp. 42–49.

19. Department of State, op. cit., item 9A.

20. UNCTAD V, Resolution 131(V), "Protectionism and Structural Adjustment."

21. Official U.S. source, June 1979.

22. UNCTAD, "The Multilateral Trade Negotiations," TD/227 (Geneva: April 2, 1979).

23. UNCTAD, "Arusha Programme," pp. 30–35.

24. Martin M. McLaughlin and Staff of the Overseas Development Council, *The U.S. and World Development: Agenda for Action, 1979* (New York: Praeger, 1979), Annex C, Table C-11, p. 218.

25. UNCTAD, "Commodities: Integrated Program for Commodities, Review of Implementation, and Follow-up Action," TD/228 (Geneva: March 12, 1979), and UNCTAD, "Action on Export Earnings Stabilization and Developmental Aspects of Commodity Policy," TD/229 (Geneva: March 8, 1979).

26. UNCTAD, "Arusha Programme," pp. 36–41.

27. Department of State, op. cit., item 10.

28. UNCTAD, "Comprehensive Measures Required to Expand and Diversify Export Trade of Developing Countries in Manufactures and Semi-manufactures," TD/230 (Geneva: February 17, 1979).

29. UNCTAD, "Arusha Programme," pp. 42–49.

30. Department of State, op. cit., item 11A.

31. UNCTAD, "Principles and Rules and Other Issues Relating to Restrictive Business Practices," TD/231 (Geneva: January 8, 1979).

32. Department of State, op. cit., item 11B.

33. UNCTAD, "Review and Evaluation of the Generalized System of Preferences," TD/232 (Geneva: January 9, 1979).

34. Department of State, op. cit., item 10.

35. UNCTAD, "International Monetary Issues," TD/233 (Geneva: March 8, 1979).

36. UNCTAD, "Arusha Programme," pp. 50–54.

37. Department of State, op. cit., item 12A, p. 4.

38. Official U.S. source, June 1979.

39. UNCTAD, "International Financial Cooperation for Development: Current Policy Issues," TD/234 (Geneva: February 9, 1979).

40. UNCTAD, "Arusha Programme," pp. 54–58.

41. Department of State, op. cit., item 12A.

42. UNCTAD V, Resolution 129(V), "The Transfer of Real Resources to Developing Countries."

43. Official U.S. source, April 4, 1979.

44. UNCTAD, "Provisional Agenda for the Fifth Session of the United Nations Conference on Trade and Development," TD/220 (Geneva: April 12, 1979), and UNCTAD, "International Financial Cooperation for Development."

45. Department of State, op. cit., item 12C.

46. UNCTAD, "International Financial Cooperation for Development."

47. UNCTAD, "Arusha Programme," p. 59.

48. Overseas Development Institute, "Debt and the Third World," Briefing Paper no. 3 (London: July 1978); and McLaughlin and Staff of ODC, op. cit.

49. Brian G. Crowe, "International Public Lending and American Policy," (Paper prepared for Office of Monetary Affairs, Bureau of Economic Affairs, Department of State, Washington, D.C., 1979).

50. Official U.S. source, September 18, 1979.

51. Ibid.

52. OECD, op. cit., p. 13.

53. Official U.S. source, June 1979.

54. UNCTAD, "Towards an Effective System of International Financial Cooperation," TD/235 (Geneva: April 23, 1979).

55. UNCTAD, "Arusha Programme," pp. 59–61.

56. OECD, op. cit., p. 13.

57. Department of State, op. cit., item 12C.

58. Crowe, op. cit.

59. UN, General Assembly, "Declaration on the Establishment of a New International Economic Order," para. 4(b).

60. UNCTAD, "Restructuring the Legal and Juridical Environment," TD/237 (Geneva: January 29, 1979).

61. U.S., Mission, Geneva, official source, March 1979.

62. Official U.S. source, May 1979.

63. Ibid.

64. Official U.S. source, June 1979.

65. UNCTAD, "Restructuring the Legal and Juridical Environment."

66. Department of State, op. cit., item 13B.

67. Official U.S. source, June 1979.

68. UNCTAD V, Resolution 101(V), "UNCTAD's Contribution to . . . Aspects of the Industrial Property System."

69. UNCTAD, "Provisional Agenda," and UNCTAD, "Towards the Technological Transformation of the Developing Countries," TD/238 (Geneva: March 15, 1979).

70. UNCTAD, "Arusha Programme," pp. 65–67.

71. Department of State, op. cit., item 13C.

72. UNCTAD V, Resolution 112(V), "Strengthening the Technological Capacity of Developing Countries."

73. OECD, op. cit., p. 15.

74. U.S. and Group B statements at final plenary session.

75. UNCTAD, "Technology: Development Aspects of the Reverse Transfer of Technology," TD/239 (Geneva: January 29, 1979).

76. UNCTAD, "Arusha Programme," pp. 67–68.

77. Department of State, op. cit., item 13D.

78. Official U.S. source, June 1979.

79. UNCTAD, "Arusha Programme," Annex II.

80. Ibid., p. 1.

81. Ibid., p. 96.

82. UN, General Assembly, "Declaration on the Establishment of a New International Economic Order," para. 4(s).

83. Department of State, op. cit., item 18.

84. UNCTAD, "Economic Cooperation Among Developing Countries: Priority Areas for Action — Issues and Approaches," TD/244 (Geneva: April 11, 1979).

85. UNCTAD, "Arusha Programme," pp. 7–24.

86. Ibid., pp. 97–99.

87. Department of State, op. cit., item 18. (For example, UNCTAD supplied the secretariat and staffing for the Arusha meeting.)

88. UNCTAD V, Resolution 127(V), "Economic Cooperation Among Developing Countries."

89. OECD, op. cit., pp. 19–20.

90. Henry Kissinger, "Global Consensus and Economic Development," Speech to Seventh Special Session, September 1, 1975 (*Department of State Bulletin,* September 22, 1975, p. 438).

91. UNCTAD, "Outline of a Substantial New Programme of Action for the 1980's for the Least Developed Countries," TD/240 (Geneva: February 13, 1979).

92. Ibid.

93. UNCTAD, "Arusha Programme," pp. 77–84.

94. Department of State, op. cit., item 15.
95. Official U.S. source, July 1979.
96. U.S. Delegation, "US and Group B Statements."

Chapter 5

1. UNCTAD, "Opening Meeting of Unctad V hears Secretary General Waldheim," TAD/INF/1051 (Manila: May 7, 1979).
2. U.S., Embassy, Manila, "Young Address to UNCTAD V," press release, May 11, 1979 (Manila: ICA).
3. Iain Guest, *Guardian,* May 16, 1979.
4. Official U.S. sources, June 1979.
5. Ibid.
6. Department of State, "Background Information" (Washington, D.C.: April 30, 1979), "Special Section on Energy." (Unclassified position papers prepared for each substantive item of the agenda for UNCTAD V.)
7. U.S. Delegation, press statement, June 1979.
8. *New York Times,* "Text to OPEC Communique on Oil at the End of Ministerial Meeting at Geneva," June 29, 1979.
9. United States, United Kingdom, France, Federal Republic of Germany, Italy, Canada, and Japan.
10. *Time,* June 25, 1979, pp. 16, 19.
11. *Time,* July 30, 1979, p. 62.
12. U.S., Embassy, Tokyo, "Tokyo Summit Communique," cable to secretary of state, June 29, 1979.
13. Ibid., p. 1, 3 of 4.
14. Ibid., p. 3, 3 of 4.
15. Ibid. p. 5, 3 of 4.
16. James Schlesinger, "Farewell Speech," press release, August 16, 1979 (London: ICA).
17. *Guardian,* January 8, 1980.
18. H. Santa Cruz, "Rising Tide of Rural Poverty and the Reasons Why," WCARRD Report no. 1 (Rome: October 1978), p. 1.
19. Ibid.
20. Ibid., pp. 1-2.
21. Department of State, "Scope Paper for WCARRD" (Washington, D.C.: 1979), pp. 4-5. (Unclassified position paper prepared for WCARRD.)
22. Ibid., p. 7.
23. Ibid., p. 6.
24. Official U.S. source, July 1979.
25. Ibid.
26. Ibid.
27. Department of State, "Scope Paper for WCARRD," p. 3.
28. A. Gayozo, personal interview, September 13, 1979.
29. See Richard N. Cooper, undersecretary of state for economic affairs, "The

Bonn Summit and Investment in Developing Countries," Statement before subcommittees on International Economic Policy and Trade and International Relations, September 20, 1978 (*Department of State Bulletin,* November 1978, pp. 19–22); and Robert Hormats, deputy assistant secretary of state for economic and business affairs (EB) speaking as chief U.S. representative to the First Meeting of the Preparatory Committee for the New International Development Strategy, April 3, 1979 (unpublished report), pp. 2–3.

30. Department of State, "Scope Paper for WCARRD," p. 7.

31. Simon Bourgin, "Walsh McDermott on the 1963 and 1979 UN S&T Conference," memorandum, November 3, 1977.

32. Department of State, "UNCSTD Scope Paper" (Washington, D.C.: August 1979), p. 13. (Unclassified position paper prepared for UNCSTD.)

33. Ibid.

34. J. W. McDonald, Jr., "Committee II—Final Wrap-up," memorandum, September 4, 1979.

35. Department of State, "List of Delegates to UNCSTD" (Washington, D.C.: August 1979).

36. Department of State, "UNCSTD Scope Paper," pp. 5–5A.

37. Ibid., pp. 6–8.

38. Ibid., pp. 9–11.

39. McDonald, op. cit.

40. Ibid.

41. Ibid.

42. Department of State, "UNCSTD Scope Paper," Target Area B.

43. Ibid.

44. Non-Aligned Countries, "Final Declaration," Conference of Heads of State or Government of Non-Aligned Countries, Conf. 6/C.2 Doc.1/Rev.3 (Havana: September 3–9, 1979).

45. *US News and World Report,* June 18, 1979, p. 28; *Washington Post,* September 9, 1979, p. A9; *US News and World Report,* September 10, 1979, p. 19.

46. Comment to the author, September 16, 1979.

Chapter 6

1. The General Assembly created the COW in 1977 (Resolution 32/174) to succeed the CIEC and to prepare for the NIEO review at the Special Session called for in 1980.

2. Resolution 34/139 was the watered-down product of an ill-timed and uncoordinated effort by Mexican President Portillo to have the United Nations initiate discussion solely on energy, which conflicted with Resolution 24/138 and was opposed by OPEC.

3. Cyrus Vance, Speech to the Thirty-fourth General Assembly, September 24, 1979.

4. Jimmy Carter, "Soviet Invasion of Afghanistan," Department of State *Current Policy Series* no. 123 (Washington, D.C.: January 1980).

5. "General Assembly Acts on Soviet Invasion," Department of State *Current Policy Series* no. 128 (Washington, D.C.: January 1980).

6. *Time,* December 24, 1979.

7. The Message was a detailed seventy-five-page document expanding on the domestic as well as the foreign policy aspects of the shorter Address (see "State of the Union," January, 24, 1980, "State of the Union Message," January 22, 1980, "Commentary by Alex Sullivan," press releases [London: ICA, January 1980]).

8. *Time,* February 4, 1980, pp. 12–16.

9. "Commentary by Alex Sullivan."

10. UNIDO was created in 1966 as an autonomous agency under the General Assembly to promote the industrial development of developing countries.

11. UNIDO, "Annotated Provisional Agenda," ID/Conf.4/1/Add.1 (Vienna: January 11, 1980).

12. UNIDO, "Industrial Development," ID/Conf.4/CRP.15 (New Delhi: January 25, 1980); Group B position paper produced by the OECD Secretariat.

13. Department of State, "Scope Paper for UNIDO III" (Washington, D.C.: January 16, 1980).

14. Committee 1: world industrial evaluation; policies aimed at achieving the Lima target; actions on behalf of the least developed, etc.; appropriate industrial structures; and foreign investment. Committee 2: energy, human resources, industrial technology, consultations, and institutional arrangements.

15. John W. McDonald, Jr., "Report of the US Delegation to the Third General Conference of the UN Industrial Development Organization (UNIDO)" (Washington, D.C.: May 2, 1980), pp. 10–14.

16. Ibid., p. 16.

17. Ibid., pp. 17–18.

18. Ibid. p. 27.

19. Ibid. p. 46.

20. Independent Commission on International Development Issues (ICIDI), *North-South: A Programme for Survival,* London: Pan Books, 1980.

21. Department of State, "Progress Report on North-South Issues" (Washington, D.C.: May 15, 1980).

22. Department of State, official source, September 1980.

23. See UNCTAD, UN Conference on Restrictive Business Practices, "The Set of Multilaterally Agreed Equitable Principles and Rules for the Control of Restrictive Business Practices," TD/RPB/Conf/10 (Geneva: September 1980).

24. Department of State, "Progress Report on North-South Issues."

25. UNCTAD, "Breakthrough on Control of Restrictive Business Practices," *Monthly Bulletin* 162 (June 1980), p. [4].

26. UNCTAD, UN Negotiating Conference on the Common Fund, "Negotiation of a Common Fund Pursuant to Conference Resolution 93(IV) on the IPC Draft Agreement Establishing the Common Fund for Commodities" (Geneva: June 26, 1980).

27. UNCTAD, "Last Month," *Monthly Bulletin* 164 (August 1980), p. [2].

28. Department of State, official source, September 1980.

29. UNCTAD, "Issues Before the Second Session of the UN Conference on an International Code of Conduct on the Transfer of Technology," press release, October 26, 1979 (Geneva: TAD/INF/1108).

30. UNCTAD, "Last Month," *Monthly Bulletin* 162 (June 1980), pp. [1–2]; Department of State, "Progress Report on North-South Issues."

31. Department of State, official source, September 1980.

32. The six-year negotiations on the Law of the Sea concluded in late August 1980, a monumental achievement, and a draft treaty was produced consisting of 180 pages, 300 articles, and 8 annexes. The draft treaty provides for DC commitments to a system of transfer of technology and compensatory payment to the LDCs, in which many observers "thought they saw the beginnings of the NIEO" (*Time,* September 8, 1980, p. 42).

33. Department of State, official source, September 1980; "North-South Dialogue," Department of State *Current Policy Series* no. 182 (Washington, D.C.: May 15, 1980).

34. Department of State, official source, September 1980.

35. UN, "Economic Committee Concludes Final Session by Deciding that Special General Assembly Meet August–September, Fails to Agree on Global Economic Negotiations Procedures," press release, July 4, 1980 (New York: GA/EC/65).

36. Ibid.

37. For a full account of the proceedings of the COW, see UN General Assembly, *Official Records,* Thirty-fourth Session, Supplement No. 34 (A 34/34); and "Summary Records" of thirty-sixth to fiftieth meetings of the COW (A/AC.191/SR 36-50), January 2–June 23, 1980.

38. Frank Balance, "Foreign Aid: Up Against the Budget Ceiling," UNA-USA, *International Report* (Summer 1980), pp. 1–2.

39. U.S., International Development Cooperation Agency, "Congressional Presentation, FY 1981" (Washington, D.C.: February 1980).

40. Department of State, "North-South Dialogue," pp. 10–12.

41. Warren Christopher, "Resources and Foreign Policy," Department of State *Current Policy Series* no. 185 (Washington, D.C.: May, 28, 1980).

42. Edmund Muskie, "The Costs of Leadership," Department of State *Current Policy Series* no. 196 (Washington, D.C.: July 7, 1980).

43. The United States is not the only delinquent. Saudi Arabia and Kuwait refused to finance more credits to the IMF's $7.8-billion Supplementary Finance Facility, then two-thirds depleted, unless it granted observer status to the PLO at the annual joint meeting of the IMF/IBRD on September 30, 1980. The United States has opposed PLO admittance on the grounds that Congress would reject legislation authorizing a $3.4-billion, three-year contribution to IDA. OPEC's move would curtail the IMF recycling of surplus oil revenues to LDCs most seriously affected by oil deficits (*New York Times,* September 5, 1980, pp. B1–B5).

44. *Time,* June 30, 1980, p. 11.

45. "Summit Statements—Afghanistan," *Department of State Bulletin* 80:2041 (August 1980), p. 7.

46. *Time,* June 30, 1980, p. 11.

47. Venice Summit, "Declaration," *Department of State Bulletin* 80:2041 (August 1980), pp. 8–11.

48. *Time,* July 7, 1980, pp. 10–12.

49. See Chapter 1, "Recapitulation."

50. UN, General Assembly, Eleventh Special Session, "Draft Annotated Agenda," A/S-11/15/ Add. 1 (August 22, 1980), and "Agenda," A/S-20 (August 25, 1980).

51. UN, General Assembly, Ad Hoc Committee of the Eleventh Special Session, "Procedures and Time-frame for the Global Negotiations, Proposal Submitted by the Chairman of Working Group II," A/S-11/AC.1/L.1 (Rev. 1) (September 5, 1980).

52. Department of State, official sources, September 1980.

53. Ibid.

54. Ibid.

55. UN, General Assembly, Eleventh Special Session, "International Development Strategy for the Third Development Decade," A/S-11/AC.1/L.2 (September 10, 1980).

56. U.S., Mission to the United Nations, "U.S. Delegation to the 11th Special Session on Development," press release, August 25, 1980 (New York: 90 [80]).

57. Department of State, official sources, September 1980.

58. *Washington Post,* October 1, 1980, p. A10.

59. Richard N. Cooper, "Statement by Undersecretary of State for Economic Affairs Before the Senate Foreign Relations Committee," September 24, 1980 (undelivered).

Chapter 7

1. Jimmy Carter, "America's Role in a Turbulent World," Department of State *Current Policy Series* no. 57 (Washington, D.C.: March 1979).

2. Cyrus Vance, "Meeting the Challenge of a Changing World," press release, May 2, 1979 (London: U.S. Embassy).

3. Daniel P. Moynihan, *A Dangerous Place* (London: Secker & Warburg, 1979), pp. 10–11.

4. Agency for International Development, "U.S. Economic Assistance, Military Assistance, and Credit Sales," AID/PPC/PB (March 1980).

5. Non-Aligned Countries, "Final Declaration," Conference of Heads of State or Government of Non-Aligned Countries, Conf.6/C.2 Doc.1/Rev.3 (Havana: September 3–9, 1979), para. 6.

6. There were nineteen congressional delegates at the Seventh Special Session; eight at UNCTAD IV; none at UNCTAD V.

7. General Accounting Office, Comptroller General, "U.S. Participation in International Organizations and Update," Report to the Congress, ID-79-26 (Washington, D.C.: August 10, 1979), pp. 2–3.

8. Office of Management and Budget, "Foreign Aid Retrenchment" (January 1981), as reported in *Washington Post,* January 29, 1981, pp. A1–A3.

Conclusions

1. Michael Manley, "North-South Dialogue," *Third World Quarterly* (October 1979), p. xxii.

2. K. G. Vaidya, "The Paris Episode in the North-South Dialogue (Paper written for Centre for Research on the New International Economic Order, Oxford, June 2, 1979).

3. Council on Environmental Quality and Department of State, *Global 2000: Entering the Twenty-First Century,* Report to the president prepared under the direction of Dr. Gerald O. Barney, 3 vols.: Vol. 1, *The Summary Report;* Vol. 2, *The Technical Report;* Vol. 3, *The Government's Global Model* (Washington, D.C.: Government Printing Office, 1980–1981). A study of the probable changes in the world's population, natural resources, and environment through the end of the century to serve as a foundation for longer-term planning.

Selected Bibliography

Books

Acheson, Dean. *Present at the Creation.* London: Hamish Hamilton, 1970.

Ashworth, William. *A Short History of International Economy Since 1850.* 3rd ed. London: Longmans, 1975.

Ball, George. *Diplomacy for a Crowded World.* London: Bodley Head, 1976.

Bhagwati, Jagdish N. *The NIEO: The North-South Debate.* Cambridge, Mass: M.I.T. Press, 1977.

Bijli, Shah M. *Developing Nations and the UNCTAD.* Aligarh: International Book Traders, 1973.

Brandon, Henry. *The Retreat of American Power.* London: Bodley Head, 1972.

Brunner, Karl, ed. *The First World, the Third World.* Rochester, N.Y.: University of Rochester, 1978.

Cline, William R. *International Monetary Reform and the Developing Countries.* Washington, D.C.: Brookings Institution, 1976.

Cohen, Saul B. *Geography and Politics in a World Divided.* 2nd ed. New York: Oxford University Press, 1975.

Connelly, Philip, and Perlman, Robert. *The Politics of Scarcity.* London: Oxford University Press, 1975.

Edberg, Rolf. *On the Shred of a Cloud.* University, Ala.: University of Alabama Press, 1966.

Fried, Edward R., and Schultze, Charles L., eds. *Higher Oil Prices and the World Economy.* Washington, D.C.: Brookings Institution, 1975.

Hansen, Roger D. *Beyond the North-South Stalemate.* New York: McGraw-Hill, 1979.

Hudson, Michael. *Global Fracture.* New York: Harper & Row, 1977.

Independent Commission on International Development Issues (ICIDI). *North-South: A Programme for Survival.* London: Pan Books, 1980.

LaFeber, Walter. *America, Russia, and the Cold War 1945–1975.* 3rd ed. New York: John Wiley and Sons, 1976.

Louis, William Roger. *Imperialism at Bay: The U.S. and the Decolonization of the British Empire 1941–1945.* Oxford: Oxford University Press, 1977.

Manubhai, Shah. *The Developing Countries and UNCTAD.* Bombay: Vora and Co., 1968.

Menon, Bhashkar P. *Global Dialogue: The New International Order.* Oxford: Pergamon Press, 1977.

Miller, J.D.B. *The Politics of the Third World.* London: Oxford University Press, 1966.

Millis, Walter, ed. *The Forrestal Diaries.* New York: Viking Press, 1951.

Moynihan, Daniel P. *A Dangerous Place.* London: Secker & Warburg, 1979.

Overseas Development Council. (James W. Howe and Staff of the ODC). *The U.S. and World Development: Agenda for Action, 1975.* New York: Praeger Publishers, 1975.

————. (Roger D. Hansen and Staff of the ODC). *The U.S. and World Development: Agenda for Action, 1976.* New York: Praeger Publishers, 1976.

————. (John W. Sewell and Staff of the ODC). *The U.S. and World Development: Agenda for Action, 1977.* New York: Praeger Publishers, 1977.

————. (Martin M. McLaughlin and Staff of the ODC). *The U.S. and World Development: Agenda for Action, 1979.* New York: Praeger Publishers, 1979.

Resources for the Future. *Resources for an Uncertain Future.* Edited by Charles Hitch. Baltimore, Md.: Johns Hopkins University Press, 1978.

Robertson, Charles L. *International Politics Since World War II.* 2nd ed. New York: John Wiley and Sons, 1975.

Rothstein, Robert L. *Global Bargaining: UNCTAD and the Quest for a New International Economic Order.* Princeton, N.J.: Princeton University Press, 1979.

Singham, A. W., ed. *The Non-Aligned Movement in World Politics.* Westport, Conn.: Laurence Holt and Co., 1977.

Spero, John Edelman. *The Politics of International Economic Relations.* London: George Allen & Unwin, 1977.

Trezise, Philip H. *The Atlantic Connection: Prospects, Problems, and Policies.* Washington, D.C.: Brookings Institution, 1975.

Willetts, Peter. *The Non-Aligned Movement.* London: Frances Pinter, 1978.

Worsely, Peter. *The Third World.* London: Weidenfeld and Nicolson, 1964.

Wriggins, W. Howard, and Adler-Karlsson, Gunnar. *Reducing Global Inequities.* New York: McGraw-Hill Book Co., 1978.

Public Documents

Commonwealth Secretariat. *The Common Fund.* Report of the Commonwealth Technical Group, September 1977. London: Commonwealth Secretariat, 1977.

European Communities Commission. "The Community and the Tokyo Round." Background Report. SEC/B53/79. London: December 13, 1979.

Food and Agriculture Organization. "Land, Food, and People." Background Report for World Conference on Agricultural Reform and Rural Development, No. 1 (October 1978), No. 2 (November 1978), No. 3 (December 1978), and No. 5 (June 1979). Rome: Food and Agriculture Organization, 1978–1979.

International Wheat Council. "First Meeting (1977/78) 1 Preparatory Group 28th September–7th October 1977." PREP (77)7. London: September 28, 1977.

————. "Eighty-sixth Session and Conference." Press release CL 86/15. London: March 23, 1979.

Non-Aligned Countries. "Final Declaration." Conference of Heads of State or Government of Non-Aligned Countries, September 3–9, 1979. NAC/Conf. 6/C.2

Doc.1/Rev.3. Havana: 1979. Reprinted in Willets, Peter. *The Non-Aligned in Havana.* London: Frances Pinter, 1980.

Organization for Economic Cooperation and Development (OECD). "The International Energy Agency." Paris: 1977.

_____. "UNCTAD Fifth Session." CES/UN(79)15. Paris: June 13, 1979.

UN, Geneva. "Head of World Food Council Appeals for Compromise on Wheat." Press release FC/30. Geneva: February 9, 1979.

UN, New York. "Provisional Agenda." UN Conference on Science and Technology for Development. A/Conf. 81/1. New York: June 20, 1979.

_____. "S&T Conference Adopts Programme of Action." Press release TEC/392. New York: September 4, 1979.

_____. "UN Conference on S&T for Development Concludes with Adoption of Action Program." Press release TEC/393. New York: September 4, 1979.

UNCTAD. "The Developing Countries and Manufactures." *Unctad IV and Beyond.* Background paper no. 1. TAD/INF/76.7. Geneva: 1976.

_____. "Negotiating Conference on Common Fund Suspended." Press release TAD/INF/904. Geneva: December 2, 1977.

_____. "The Debt Problem." Unctad IV and Beyond. Background paper no. 3. TAD/INF/PUB/78.1. Geneva: February 1978.

_____. "Code of Conduct for Transfer of Technology." *Unctad IV and Beyond.* Background paper no. 4. TAD/INF/PUB/78.3. Geneva: July 1978.

_____. "Notification." Letter from UNCTAD Secretary-General Corea to members. TDO 254/2. Geneva: January 29, 1979.

_____. *Monthly Bulletin* 151–159. Geneva: April 1979–March 1980.

_____. Basic Documentation for UNCTAD V, Series TD/220–245. Geneva: May 1979.

_____. "Issues Before 2nd Session of the UN Conference on an International Code of Conduct on Transfer of Technology." Press release TAD/INF/1108. Geneva: October 26, 1979.

U.S., Congress. "Report by Congressional Advisers to the Seventh Special Session of the UN." Washington, D.C.: October 9, 1975.

U.S., Department of State. *Department of State Bulletin.* Washington, D.C.: Government Printing Office.

"The Global Challenge and International Cooperation." Address by Secretary Kissinger, August 4, 1975, pp. 149–157.

"Global Consensus and Economic Development." Address by Secretary Kissinger. September 22, 1975, pp. 425–441.

"UNCTAD IV: Expanding Cooperation for Global Economic Development." Address to UNCTAD IV by Secretary Kissinger, Nairobi, May 6, 1976. May 31, 1976, pp. 657–672.

"Department Discusses Results of CIEC Meeting." Richard N. Cooper. July 18, 1977, pp. 92–99.

_____. *U.S. Participation in the UN.* Washington, D.C.: Government Printing Office.

Pub. 8880, 10 and Conf. Series 124, Year 1975 (Pub. 1976).

Pub. 8916, 10 and Conf. Series 129, Year 1976 (Pub. 1977).

Pub. 8964, 10 and Conf. Series 137, Year 1977 (Pub. 1978).

————. Report of the U.S. Delegation to the Second General Conference of the UN Industrial Development Organization (UNIDO), Lima, Peru, March 12–27, 1975. W. Tapley Bennett, Jr., Chairman. Unpublished.

————. "International Investment and Multinational Enterprises." OECD Guidelines. Washington, D.C.: 1976.

————. "Report of the U.S. Delegation to the United Nations Conference on Trade and Development (UNCTAD), Fourth Session, Nairobi, Kenya, May 5–31, 1976. Paul H. Boeker, Chairman. Unpublished.

————. "The United States and the Third World." General Foreign Policy Series no. 301, publication no. 8863. Washington, D.C.: Government Printing Office, 1976.

————. "Walsh McDermott on the 1963 and 1979 UN S&T Conference." Memorandum dated November 3, 1977, by Simon Bourgin. Unpublished: in possession of the author.

————. "International Public Lending and American Policy." Study by Brian G. Crowe, Office of Monetary Affairs, 1979. Unpublished: in possession of the author.

————. *Science and Technology for Development.* U.S. national paper for UNCSTD. Publication 8966, 10 and Conf. Series 139. Washington, D.C.: Government Printing Office, 1979.

————. *Gist.* Washington, D.C.: Bureau of Public Affairs.

"The MTNs." March 1979.

"Foreign Indebtedness of the U.S. Government." April 1979.

————. "America's Role in a Turbulent World." Speech by President Carter. (Department of State) *Current Policy Series* no. 57. Washington, D.C.: Bureau of Public Affairs, March 1979.

————. "America's Commitment to Third World Development." Speech by Secretary Vance. *Secretary of State.* Washington, D.C.: Bureau of Public Affairs, March 30, 1979.

————. "A Guide to UNCTAD V Monetary and Financial Issues." Report no. 1162. Washington, D.C.: Bureau of Intelligence Research, April 17, 1979.

————. Instructions to U.S. delegations to UNCTAD V, Manila, May 1979; World Conference on Agrarian Reform and Rural Development, Rome, July 1979; and UN Conference on Science and Technology for Development, Vienna, Austria, August 1979. Unpublished.

————. "America and the Developing World." Address by Secretary Vance. (Department of State) *Current Policy Series* no. 75. Washington, D.C.: Bureau of Public Affairs, July 1979.

————. "Committee II — Final Wrap-up." Memorandum dated September 4, 1979, by John W. McDonald, Jr. Unpublished: in possession of the author.

————. Delegation lists of U.S. delegations to various North-South conferences since the Seventh Special Session. Unpublished: in possession of the author.

U.S., Embassy, London. Press releases. ICA.

"Meeting the Challenge of a Changing World." Address by Secretary of State Vance. May 2, 1979.

"Farewell Speech" by Energy Secretary Schlesinger. August 16, 1979.

"Carter Maps Steady Course to Meet New Challenges: State of the Union Message." January 22, 1980.

"State of the Union." President Carter's Address to Congress. January 24, 1980.

U.S., General Accounting Office, Comptroller General. "U.S. Participation in International Organizations, an Update." Report to the Congress. Washington, D.C.: 1979.

U.S., Mission to the UN, New York. "Statement by Robert Hormats, Chief U.S. Representative to the Preparatory Committee for the New International Development Strategy, April 3, 1979." Press release USUN-35(79). New York: 1979.

World Bank. *World Development Report.* New York: Oxford University Press, 1978.

―――. *1979 Annual Report.* Washington, D.C.: World Bank, 1979.

Reports, Papers, and Lectures

Aspen Institute for Humanistic Studies. *The Planetary Bargain.* Princeton, N.J.: Aspen Institute, 1976.

Atlantic Council of the United States. *Beyond Diplomacy.* Washington, D.C.: Atlantic Council, 1976.

Centre for Research on the NIEO. *North-South Negotiations: Review and Prospects.* Oxford: Centre for Research on the NIEO, 1978.

Congressional Research Service. *The Soviet Union and the Third World: A Watershed in Great Power Conflict.* Report to the Committee on International Relations, House of Representatives. Washington, D.C.: Government Printing Office, 1977.

Mathieson, John. "The Tokyo Round Trade Agreement: What Effect on Developing Countries?" *Communique.* Washington: Overseas Development Council, March 1979.

Overseas Development Institute. Briefing Paper Series. London.

Paris Conference on International Economic Cooperation. No number. 1976.

The Textile Trade, Developing Countries, and the Multi-Fiber Agreement. No Number. 1976.

Debt and the Third World. No. 3. 1978.

Whither the Common Fund. No. 4. 1978.

Basic Needs. No. 5. 1978.

The Tokyo Round and Developing Countries. No number. September 1979.

Compensatory Finance to Stabilize Export Earnings. No. 1. 1979.

Agrarian Reform. No. 3. 1979.

Schweitzer, Pierre-Paul. *The IMF and Its Role.* Stamp Memorial Lecture. London: Athlone Press, 1969.

Watson, Paul. *Debt and the Developing Countries: New Problems and New Actions.* Devel-

opment Paper no. 26, NIEO Series. Washington, D.C.: Overseas Development
Council, 1978.

Wessels, Wolfgang, ed. *Europe and the North-South Dialogue.* Atlantic Papers no. 35.
Paris: Atlantic Institute for International Affairs, 1978.

Articles

Amuzegar, Jahangir. "A Requiem for the North-South Conference." *Foreign Affairs,*
56:1 (October, 1977), pp. 136–159.

Leiber, Robert J. "Europe and America in the World Energy Crisis." *International
Affairs* 55:4 (October 1979), pp. 531–545.

Ramphal, Shridath S. "The North-South Dialogue." *Third World Quarterly,* 1:1 (January 1979), pp. 1–17.

Yanchinski, Stephanie. "UNCSTD and After." *New Scientist,* September 6, 1979, pp.
724–726.

Unpublished Material

Johnson, Joel. Letter to author dated November 28, 1979. Johnson is a member of
the Policy Planning Staff of the State Department and was the officer with principal responsibility for drafting and coordinating Secretary Vance's speech at
Seattle, March 30, 1979.

Sewell, John W., and Mathieson, John A. "What Are America's Interests in Third
World Development?" Paper prepared for the Conference on Rich Country Interests in Third World Development, University of Sussex, November 14–17,
1979.

Vaidya, K. G. "The Paris Episode in the North-South Dialogue." Paper delivered
to seminar on North-South negotiations in the CIEC at Queen Elizabeth House,
Oxford, June 2, 1979, sponsored by Centre for Research on the New International Economic Order.

Index